"You have to live it to understand it."

- Rolling Thunder

Copyright © 2000 by Mark C. Billington and Joe Flynn

Published by Vantage Press, Inc.
516 West 34th Street, New York, New York 10001

Manufactured in the United States of America
ISBN: 0-533-13542-7

Library of Congress Catalog Card No.: 00-90931

0 9 8 7 6 5 4 3 2 1

SEARCH FOR AH...

The Myth of Modern Music

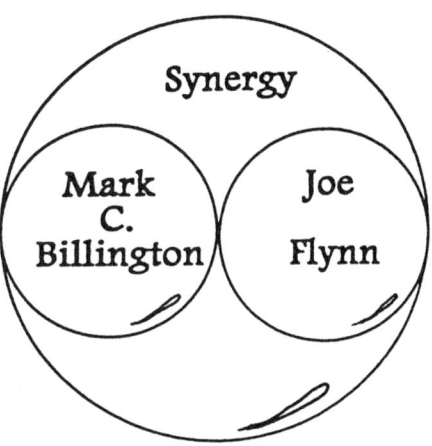

Most Illustrations by Kristi Rose Turman

Map, Waves, Boxes & other Drawings by J. Flynn

VANTAGE PRESS

New York

For

Ammah Joy

"How incredible to be described
are these bright points
which appear in the blue sky
as the darkness increases,
said to be other worlds,
like berries on the hills
when the summer is ripe!"
- H. D. Thoreau

Contents

All characters are fictional. Pytag dreams Pythagorean mathematics
& is not meant to portray the historical Pythagoras.

Preface

The history of Western music is largely understood as how the 12 pitches per octave found on modern piano keyboards have been put to use. However, long before there were pianos, musicians struggled with how to divide the octave into functional units that could combine harmoniously yet provide sufficient musical complexity. The theories and practical applications which these musicians developed are known as tuning systems.

The earliest records of research in the area of tuning systems focus on work by Pythagoras, the ancient Greek whose work in Geometry led to the well known Pythagorean Theorem (a formula for calculating the lengths of the sides of right triangles). It was Pythagoras' investigation of the natural harmonic series - overtones produced along with the fundamental pitch when a note is played - that led to the development of modern tuning systems. Some of these systems use as few as 5 tones per octave, while others utilize as many as 41.

For reasons that are not well documented, the majority of the Western world settled on dividing the octave into 12 pitches. Later, J. S. Bach chose to make the musical distance between those 12 pitches exactly equal (one twelfth of an octave per division). This system became known as "Equal Temperament" and it allowed musicians to modulate from one key center to another without having to re-tune their instruments. Major and Minor scales (8 pitches including the octave) were selected from these 12 pitches and they became the predominant scales used in Western music composition during the last three hundred years.

Today, many musicians are exploring historic ways to tune their instruments and new systems have also been developed. The compositions which they have created make use of the very different character of pitches which do not fall into the more familiar system of equal temperament. Joe Flynn and Mark C. Billington are among the group of musicians who were drawn to rethink the desirability of equal temperament. In Search for Ah... they offer a metaphoric explanation of earlier pitch systems and of how modern scales came to prominence. They then present their own, well thought-out suggestion for a system which uses an 8 tone scale (9 including the octave) and they explain why that makes far more "musical sense". Their scale is based upon pitches which are all found in the natural harmonic series and they expand upon that scale to define a 16 note per octave system, also based entirely upon the harmonic series.

Search for Ah... is easy to follow. It works both as an explanation of tuning systems with their resultant "families of pitches" and as an engaging adventure story set on a beautiful island. You will find it enjoyable reading and a valuable education. It is a revolutionary look at the science and aesthetics of tuning systems.

Terry A. Setter,
Senior Music Faculty
The Evergreen State College

Introduction

<u>Search for Ah...</u> is about the Harmony family.
It describes the search for a child lost in a mountain wilderness.
It is also a study of the mathematics and physics of music.
The problem is that modern music is not in alignment
with current understanding of the physics of sound.

This misalignment has been a source of confusion
for twenty-five hundred years,
since Pythagoras sought to use mathematics
to explain music.
The authors claim Pythagoras made an error.
This book is about the search for, and recovery of,
lost harmonics.

The musical and mathematical symbols in the Story
cross-reference with the Theory.
Doe, Rae, Mee, Fu, Sol, Mu, Ah and Tee
are sisters in the Harmony family.
Each character, like each musical tone, has its own unique personality.
The Story describes how they grow up and learn to sing together
with the unifying influence of their adopted brother, Song.
But a problem develops in this family;
their unity breaks down
into confusion.

Doe, Rae, Mee, Fu, Sol, Mu, Ah and Tee
represent "overtones" which are naturally occurring harmonics
(a series of specific subtle tones)
created spontaneously out of the fundamental, or original tone.
Doe is the fundamental tone.
The harmonics are each a unique, individual pitch,
as closely related as sisters.
Ah is # 7 in the series,
yet she has been left out of Western music.

- the Authors

Cast of Characters

Joon: Harmony Family Mother

Pytag: Bull Headed Father

Song: Adopted Son of the Harmony Family

Doe: Oldest Sister; Harmonic # 1, 2, 4, ⑧ 16...

Rae: # ⑨ 18, 36...

Mee: # 5, ⑩ 20, 40...

Fu: # ⑪ 22, 44...

Sol: # 3, 6, ⑫ 24...

Mu: # ⑬ 26, 52...

Ah: # 7, ⑭ 28...

Tee: Youngest Daughter: # ⑮ 30, 60...

Tom: Story-Telling Drum-Maker

Will & Flux: Twins

Omma: Queen

Art: King

Gim: Fish Taco Dood

Two Healers

Browser: Young Long-Tailed Bear
Urr: Momma Bear
Bootes: Brother Bear

Seerius: Family Dog

Yoti: Coyote

Magic: Old White Horse

Three Dolphins

On the Island of Murlyn

1. AT THE EDGE OF THE FOREST

At the Edge of the Forest

Once
a young woman
lived in a small village
at the edge of the forest
outside the Great City
of Murlyn.

Her name was Joon Harmony.

Joon loved nature.
She loved the golden glow of sunrise.
She loved flaming reds
& delicious oranges of sunset.
She loved songs of birds
& the sound of wind
in green trees.
She loved brown earth,
blue sky,
white clouds
& she loved purple berries
that grew in secret places
in the forest.

Joon was also in love with a man
who lived in a castle
in the Great City.

His name was Pytag.

The Secret of Roofs

Pytag was a hero to the people of Murlyn.
He had discovered the Secret of Roofs.

With his formula
Pytag built strong, dry houses
that protected the people
from winter rains;
for Murlyn was a northern island
& winter weather was severe.

Pytag gained fame & fortune.
His formula was written
in the Big Book of Numbers.
He was considered by the Great City people
to be the smartest man.

But it was no secret
that Pytag was proud, arrogant
& difficult to talk with.
He was so stubborn
that many people called him
"Bull Headed".

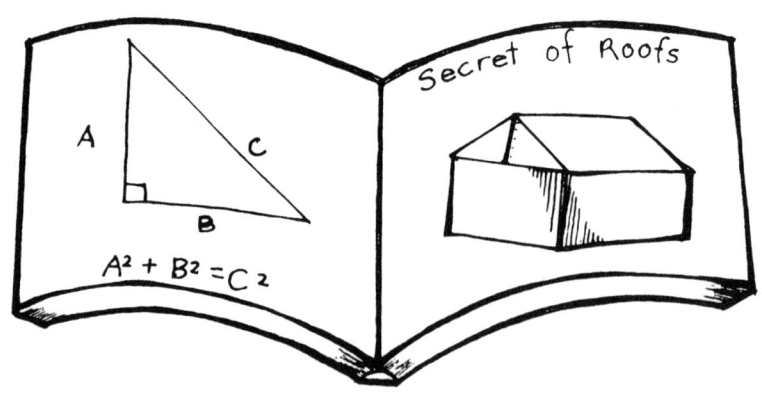

Absence of the King & Queen

The young hero, Pytag,
had influenced the people:
"You don't need a king & queen.
You can rule yourselves..."

They believed him.

Queen Omma & King Art
disappeared from the Great City
because people had stopped believing in them.

In the absence of the king & queen
Pytag moved into their castle
& supervised the building
of the Great City.

Meeting at the Well

To the Great City people
Pytag was a builder
but he envisioned himself as
a hunter.

Pytag would often leave the city
for journeys in the forest.

One day Joon was drawing water
from her village well
as Pytag passed through.

He stopped at the well
to fill his water jug.
Their eyes met
& sparkled.

After this, Pytag visited frequently.
The two began to share their inner selves.
Little by little, their love grew.

Why Joon felt such love for this man
she was not quite sure.
She did not love riches
& she did not want fame.
She did not like big, cold castles,
nor the Great City
& she did not usually like
stubborn, arrogant people.

But somehow this feeling was different.
She just couldn't help it.
She felt love.

Closer to the Forest

In time,
Pytag spoke of his deepest desires:

"I want to marry you, Joon
& share my castle with you
in the Great City."

Joon smiled inwardly.
She thought of her family & dear friends
in the small village.

She chose her words carefully:
"I will marry you, Pytag, on one condition...
I don't want to live in your castle
which is rightfully the home
of the queen & king.
My home & heart are in the village."

Pytag accepted Joon's condition.
"I'm tired of that old castle, anyway," he said.
Pytag longed to live closer to the forest
& hunt more often.

And so it came to pass that they were wed
according to an ancient Murlyn custom,
honoring mothers:
A man accepts the last name of a woman.
Joon, Pytag & any children
would be known as
the Harmony family.

By a Clear Spring

Outside the small village
Joon chose a favorite place
for their new home,
beside a spring
that trickled clear water
into a quiet pool.

Early morning sun
shining on the water
reflected off ripples
onto a wall of smooth white stone
behind the spring.

Joon called this Spring
the "Rippling Pool".
It was a place she loved
to sit, clear her thoughts
& sing,
watching reflections of ripples.

Pytag built a fine house for them
out of the white stone
common in that area.

Joon designed a courtyard
with gardens
around the Rippling Pool.

White stone steps
led from the courtyard
to bedrooms upstairs;
for they hoped
to have children someday.

A well designed roof
kept their home dry
through long, wet winters.

Song from the Forest

Before the births of their own children,
a very strange thing had happened...

One spring morning Joon awoke
& opened the front door to greet the day.

On the doorstep, in a basket,
a healthy child smiled up at her
bubbling & babbling happily.
It was a baby boy
with a voice like mountain streams.

Joon was inspired
by the liquid murmuring
of this small boy's voice.
She named him
"Song"
& raised him
as her own.

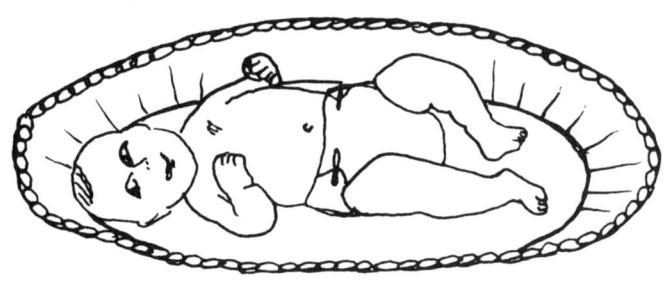

Poppers

No one seemed to know where Song was born.
They guessed
he was abandoned by forest wanderers.

The Great City people & small village folk
called forest people "Poppers"
because they ate wild food
like seeds from tallgrass plants.
They were known for their special method
of popping the tallgrass seeds over open fires,
making a tasty treat.

Even the people of the Great City
enjoyed eating popseed.

But many Great City people looked down on Poppers
because their clothes were sometimes ragged,
their hair was often tangled
& they rarely worked in the city.

Sisters

Doe,
the first daughter born to Joon & Pytag,
was named for the deer
that grazed in fields nearby.
Purple rose buds filled her heart
& rainbows reflected in her big eyes.

Rae
was named for the sunshine.
She was bright, red-orange, & warm
from the soft fire burning within her.
Quiet flames danced in her luminous eyes.

Mee
had orange hair with loose curls
around her freckled face.
Her eyes were golden yellow.
She was often silly & giggled.
This bothered Pytag.
When he scolded her, she cried & became angry.
In her, Joon & Pytag saw themselves.

Fu,
an observant child,
was named for principles in life.
She was quiet.
Yellow-green glowed in her heart
& reflected in the deep pools
of her almond shaped eyes.

Sol
was a child of change.
She flowed back & forth from green to blue.
She was active, full of desire.

Mu
was blue as late evening sky.
Her heart was blue, her eyes were blue.
Her hair was a pile of tight black curls.
She was named in honor of all Murlyn mothers.
She cared about everyone.

"Ah..."
Joon said
when her seventh daughter was born.
Ah had liquid blue-violet eyes, flowing hair,
a fluid smile
& a voice like Song's
with sounds of running water.

Like a Kite String

Song was a dreamy child,
his heart & mind flying high in the sky,
soaring like a kite in the wind.

Doe was very practical,
her feet rooted to the ground,
nourishing the Harmony family.

Doe loved everyone.
In her silent strength she was relaxed
& easy to be around.
All the Harmony children loved
to play with Doe.

Song felt lost without Doe.
In turn, Song was her inspiration.
The love between them was like a kite string
binding his heaven to her earth.

Relations

Rae was a fabulous dancer;
quick & light on her feet.
She moved so fast that no one could keep up with her,
darting around, leaping, jumping & twirling in circles.
She came & went so fast
her sisters rarely saw her.

Mee grew more dominant as the family grew.
Creative & expressive,
she loved to perform.

Fu watched the world closely.
Rarely did anyone know her thoughts,
but when she spoke
her words were always clear
& well chosen.
Fu loved to eat olives.

Sol was restless & flighty.
Doe kept her close to home.
Sol seemed inseparable from Doe,
yet dominated all her other sisters.

Mu shared her mother's tender heart.
She stayed very close to Joon,
learning.

Ah was a curious child;
always exploring
& discovering the unknown.
She was easily entertained
& satisfied with many little things.

Everyone loved Ah...

2. BY THE DANGEROUS RIVER

Seerius

One day Pytag brought home a fluffy puppy
for the children to play with.
They named him:

"Seerius".

This little ball of fluff
grew to be a great big dog.

Seerius proved faithful to the family.
He was always near one of them,
or not far away.

Called into the Forest

One fine spring day
Joon felt called into the forest.
It had been another long, wet winter.
It seemed like ages
since she had been out of doors.

She longed
to see red, orange & yellow flowers in bloom.
She yearned to hear birds singing in trees
& feel fresh wind blowing.
She wanted to pick green leaves of healing herbs
& prepare buds of certain flowers
for medicines she was learning how to use.

If she was very lucky
perhaps she might even find some purple tone berries.
That would lift her spirit
out of the long gray winter.

Most of the children were content to stay home.

The sisters had discovered their voices.
They loved nothing better
than to sing together
in their garden.

Into the Wilderness with Pytag

Song loved to walk in the forest
with his mother.
She had taught him many things
about plants, trees & flowers.

But when Pytag decided that he, a hunter,
must go along,
for this was the season
when wild beasts prowled
in search of food,
Song chose not to join them.
He felt uncomfortable with Pytag.

Song tried,
but could find little respect in his heart
for this man he believed was his father.
Song loved him
but Pytag was so arrogant, so bull headed.

Song thought,
"I would rather stay home
& make music with my sisters
than go into the wilderness
with Pytag."

From his hunting box, Pytag selected the sword
to protect Joon from wild beasts
in the forest.
They took little Ah with them.
She was too young, they thought,
to be left home.
The others were old enough
to look after themselves
for a day.

Seerius, their big dog,
would stay home with the children.

Parting Words

Pytag's parting words to Song were:
"Make sure nothing happens."

Song's reply was:
"What could possibly happen in two hours?"

"It might be more than two hours,"
Pytag warned.

"Nothing's gonna happen..."
The last words were Song's.

Into the Forest

Joon & Pytag
walked with Ah,
deep into the forest,
showing her wondrous things.

Early in the morning
dew drops sparkled
on ferns & moss
growing high in the branches
of green trees.

Ah saw faces in natural sculptures
of stone.
She felt the pulse of a nearby river
as it poured from the mountains.

The child responded
to spring's awakening
with her melodious,
"Ah..."

Red robins gathered, singing.
Many colored thrushes
hidden in tree tops
joined voices.

Blue birds were only now appearing
from distant winter homes
far south.
It was still early spring;
flowers had not yet bloomed.

A Peaceful Afternoon

All day Joon searched
but could find no herbs
or medicinal blossoms.
Joon saw no purple berries.

Joon, Pytag & Ah emerged from the forest
in late afternoon
resting in a green meadow.
A river rumbled
on the far side of this field.

Ah slept peacefully on a blanket, but
Joon wanted to walk up the river
for herbs & berries.

Joon asked Pytag,
"Will you stay with Ah?"

Pytag: "But of course dear..."

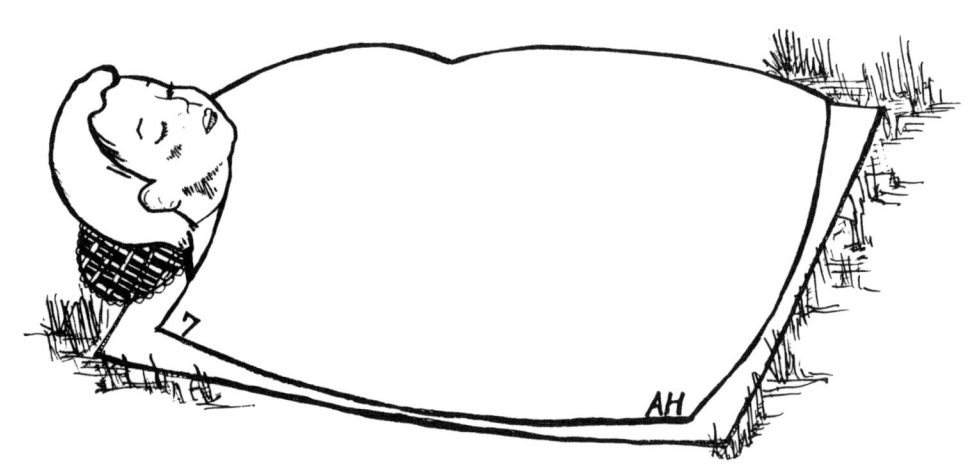

"Forbidden Fruit"

"Don't eat any of those tone berries," Pytag warned.

Joon laughed.
That's exactly what she wanted to do!

Tone berries...
their purple color, taste & energy
always enhanced her child-like awe...

"I'm serious!" Pytag said in a harsh tone.

"No, dear," Joon smiled,
"Seerius is our dog."

Pytag went on:
"You don't want to end up like those Poppers
who wander around aimlessly in the forest,
never amounting to anything.
Or worse yet,
end up like those
twin brothers of mine
hiding away in the mountains.
That's what happens to people
who eat tone berries!
Those toners..." he grumbled.

Long ago,
Pytag had convinced elders of the Great City
to declare tone berries
illegal
under the category of:
"Forbidden Fruit".

Pytag called anyone who liked tone berries,
"Toners".
He had a problem with them.
He thought tone berries made people act silly.
"People should be serious," Pytag often said.

"Now Pytag..."
Joon softened the hunter's heart;
"There is nothing wrong with tone berries...
all plants, seeds & fruits
are gifts of nature...
little purple berries
could not cause such big problems."

Beside the Rushing River

Joon walked toward the river.

Relaxing on the blanket with Ah
Pytag startled at what seemed to be
the rhythmic gallumph
of a long-tailed bear.

He grabbed up his sword
& silently pursued the sound.

Ah woke up & looked around.
She heard rushing water
& crawled toward it.

Beside the river
Ah saw a small brown bear with a long tail
eating berries.

Swept Away

"Will you play with me, Baby Bear?"
Ah bubbled with excitement.

The little bear jumped into the air,
tiny legs scrambling but going nowhere.
The bear landed, tumbling down into the rushing river.

In an instant
the little bear was swept away.

Ah shut her eyes & cried,
her mouth open wide,

"Mommaaa...
        ommaaa...
                aaahh..."

But only sounds of water
could be heard.

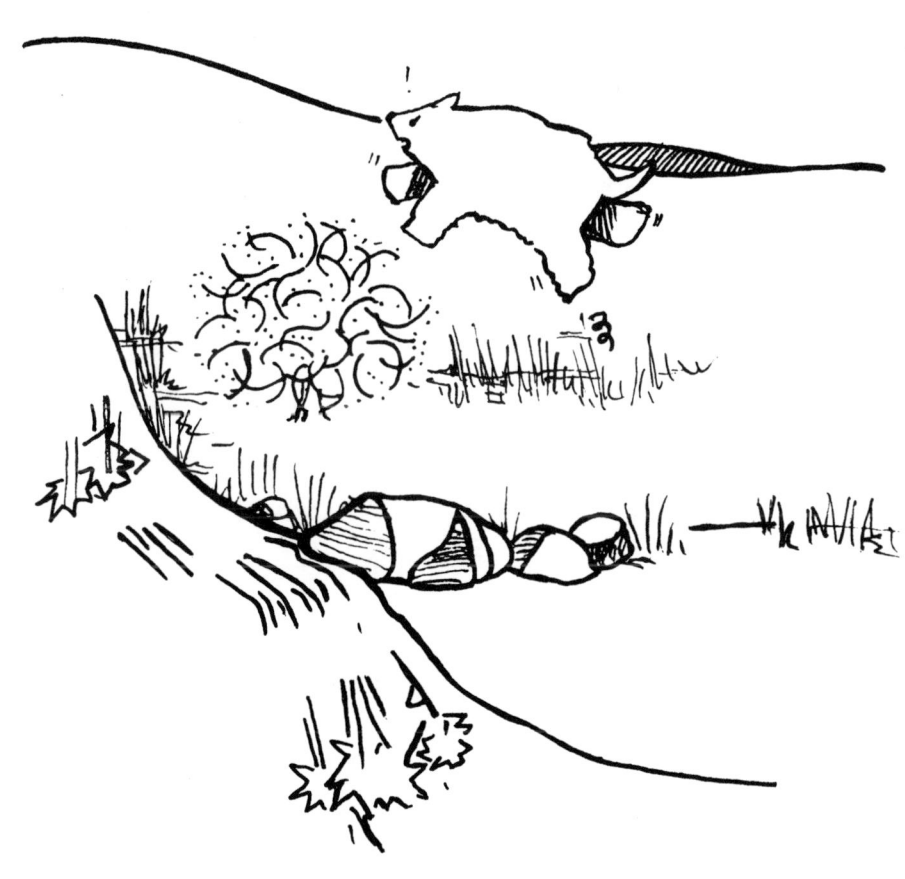

Momma Comes Running

In a sudden blur of movement...

A huge animal swept Ah off her feet
& gallumphed away with her
into the forest.

From the mouth of a momma bear
Ah hung in her blue-violet pajamas.

Momma bear was brown.
A young black bear with white feet ran behind her.
These bears had long tails, too.

For an instant
Ah saw her mother
& heard:

"Ahhh...!!"

Cut short,
Joon fell under paws & claws
of two running bears
disappearing into darkening forest
with Ah...

"What happened to Ah...?"

In less than two minutes
the world changed.

Pytag didn't know what had happened.
Ah was gone.
Joon was lying on the ground, unconscious,
bleeding from a wound
across her heart.

Pytag took Joon in his arms.
He began to sob,
"What happened Joon?
...O Joon...
What happened to Ah...?"

Pytag became dizzy & disoriented.
For a long moment
he didn't know where he was
or what to do.

He stood up heavily
with Joon in his arms.
He paced up & down the river
looking for traces of Ah...

He saw fresh tracks
down slick mud to the river,
grass bent over into rushing water.

Pytag thought the worst.

He hurried from the river
to get Joon home,
but in dim forest
he took an unfamiliar path.

In the Medicine Village

This unfamiliar path led far into the woods.
Pytag followed it to a clearing.
In the center
he saw a circle of round houses
woven from sticks
with cones of thatched grass
for roofs.

"A primitive village," Pytag thought.
He approached cautiously,
skin tingling.
Hunter's awareness surged within him.

In the center of the circle
an old man with a long gray beard
tended a fire.
A woman, bent with age,
came from a hut
carrying a kettle.

"Where am I?" Pytag asked.

"This is the Medicine Village,"
she answered, examining Joon's wound.
"What happened to this woman?"

"I don't know..." Pytag stammered.

The old man hobbled over.

The woman placed a hand on Joon's belly
& looked at Pytag...

"She is with child."

"No!" Pytag raised his voice,
"Ah is lost!
I must go & find her..."

"Do as you must," the old woman assured him.
"We will care for this woman," the old man spoke.
"Until you return," the old woman added, "fear not for her."
"The woman will heal, & the child will live,"
the old man finished.

But Pytag did not hear their words.
He hurried away.

After Darkness Fell

Pytag returned to the river.

He searched the area
where Joon had been injured.
There he found his sword.
Some of her blood was on it.

He searched
through blue twilight
into black night,
wandering far down river,
but he found no trace of Ah...

Long after darkness fell
Pytag gave up his search.

A terrible thought entered his head:

"Ah is dead!"

He could not get the thought
out of his mind.

He tried to sleep in the spring grass
but the river's tone
reminded him of Ah...

He rolled over & over restlessly,
staring into confusing patterns
of stars.

Thoughts of his fragmented family
tortured him into a troubled sleep
& he dreamed a strange dream:

One he had dreamed before...

3. PYTAG-ORION DREAM

The Hunter

In his dream
Pytag saw a familiar constellation of stars
in the clear sky of his mind:

Orion

       . . .

             the Hunter.

He saw himself in those stars;
his great sword raised high above his head
to slay a wild beast of the forest.

Three stars
of Orion's Belt
began to glow & pulsate.

Those three stars
alone
filled the sky.

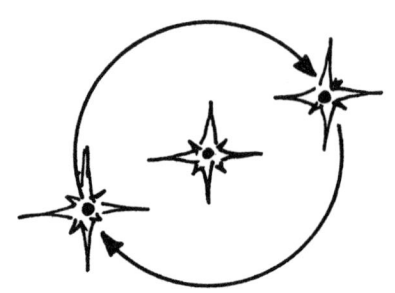

The two outer stars

began to rotate

around the center star.

Then the center star

joined in the circle

dancing

around the empty center.

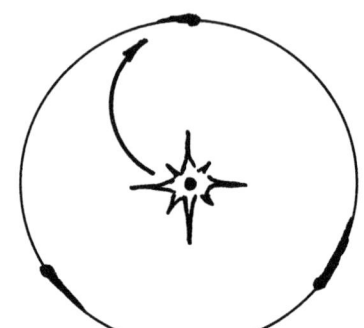

There

seemed to be nothing

inside the spinning circle.

But

Pytag saw everything...

emptiness

filled

with power & meaning.

The answers to all questions

were in there.

So he watched

closely.

30

The three spinning stars
began to shift;
each into their own path
rolling
into a loosely spun
ball
of light...

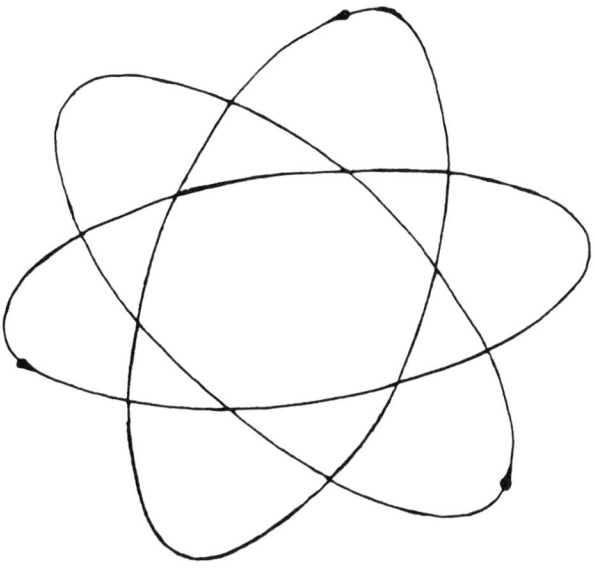

Three spinning paths
turned on their edges
& flattened into lines
touching
end to end.

These three lines
drew a perfect triangle
that filled the dark sky
in Pytag's
sleeping
eyes.

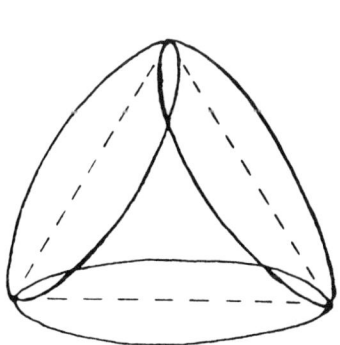

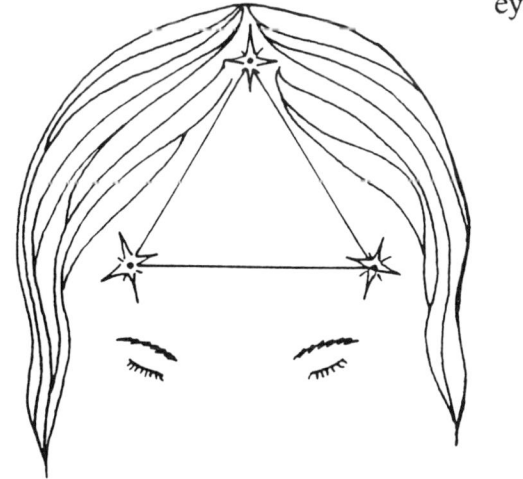

Inside of Pytag's restless mind
the stars shifted again.
The star of the right foundation
moved to the left
cutting the triangle
in half.

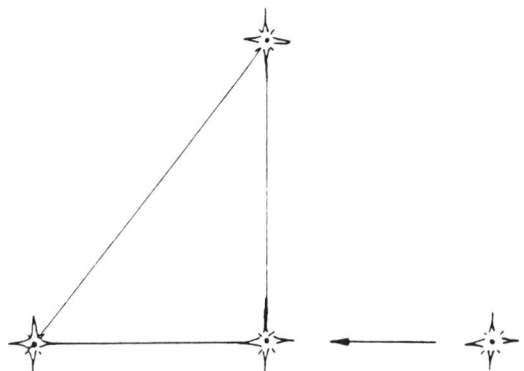

Pressure from the colliding stars
caused the triangle
to fall over.

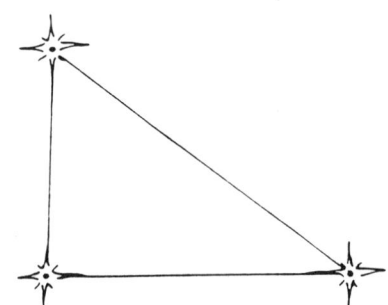

The three corner stars
continued to blaze
with meaning.

Boxes
    in patterns
        began popping
            out of the three sides
                of the triangle.

From this simple shape
    & these simple patterns
        Pytag had derived the formula
        for building
            strong, dry houses:

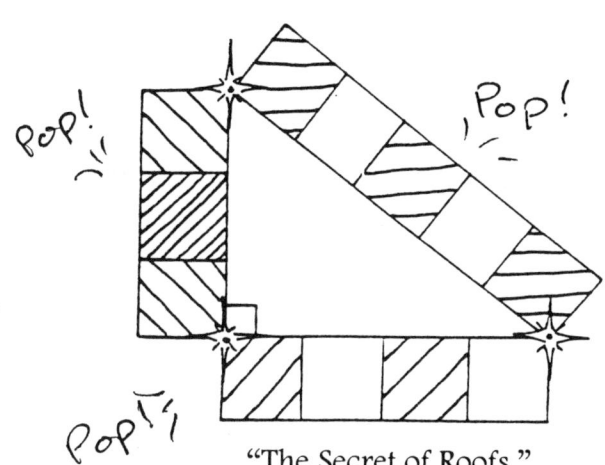

"The Secret of Roofs."

It was as simple as:

a	b	c
3	4	5

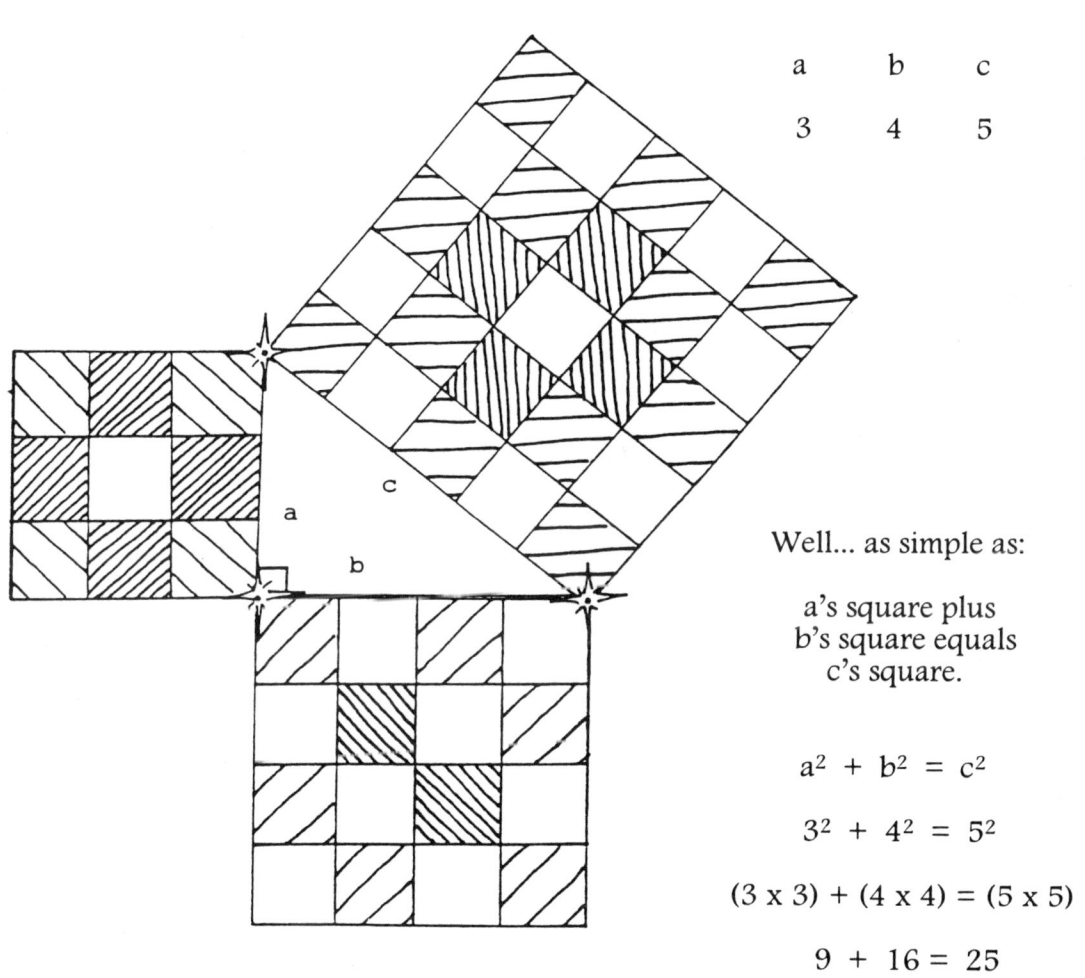

Well... as simple as:

a's square plus
b's square equals
c's square.

$$a^2 + b^2 = c^2$$

$$3^2 + 4^2 = 5^2$$

$$(3 \times 3) + (4 \times 4) = (5 \times 5)$$

$$9 + 16 = 25$$

33

Patterns

Pytag woke up with a start!

That dream again ... those patterns ....

Again & again he had dreamed that same dream.
What did it mean this time?
He thought he had figured it all out
long ago,
before he had built the strong houses of Murlyn.

"Is there more?" Pytag wondered...

Surely he could find the answer.

"1. 2.. 3..."

Pytag thought... "1. 2.. 3..."

He said it out loud: "One, two, three..."
Again & again he repeated, "One, two, three..."
until his own eyes began to glow like stars.

"1. 2.. 3..."

1. He believed that Ah was dead.
2.. He was afraid that Joon might also die.
3... He was confused.
 .
 .
 .

1. Alone.
2.. Entangled.
3...
 .
 .
 .

"1.2..3...
          1.2..3...
                    1.2.."

1 to 2

Pytag thought:

"Two is twice as large as one.
 Four is twice as large as two.
 Eight is twice as large as four...

"It's a pattern
        of doubling."

1 doubling to 2 to 4   to   8   to   16
2

4

8

16

32   & on into   infinity....

Bubbles rose

     & floated

          inside of Pytag's mind...

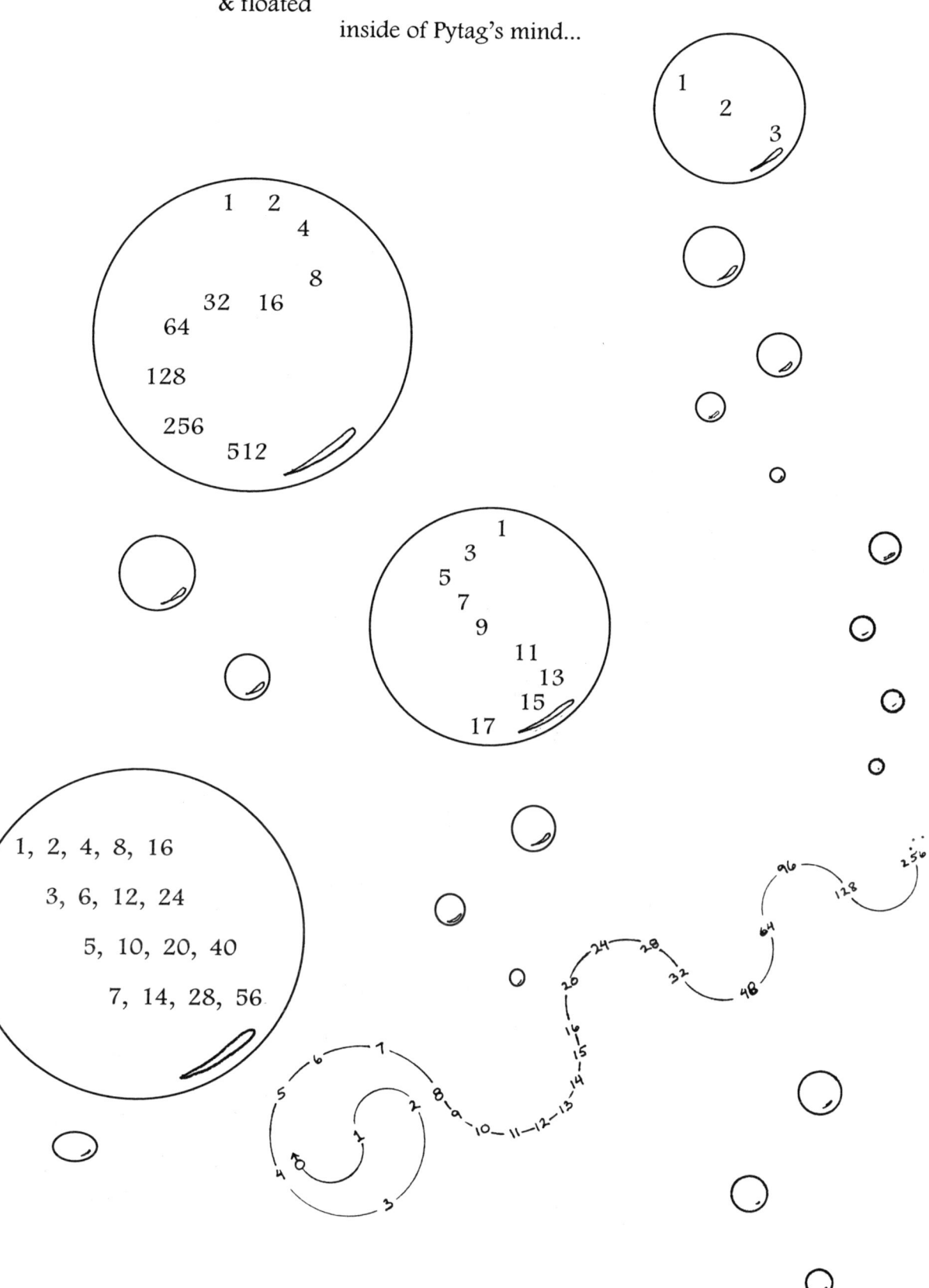

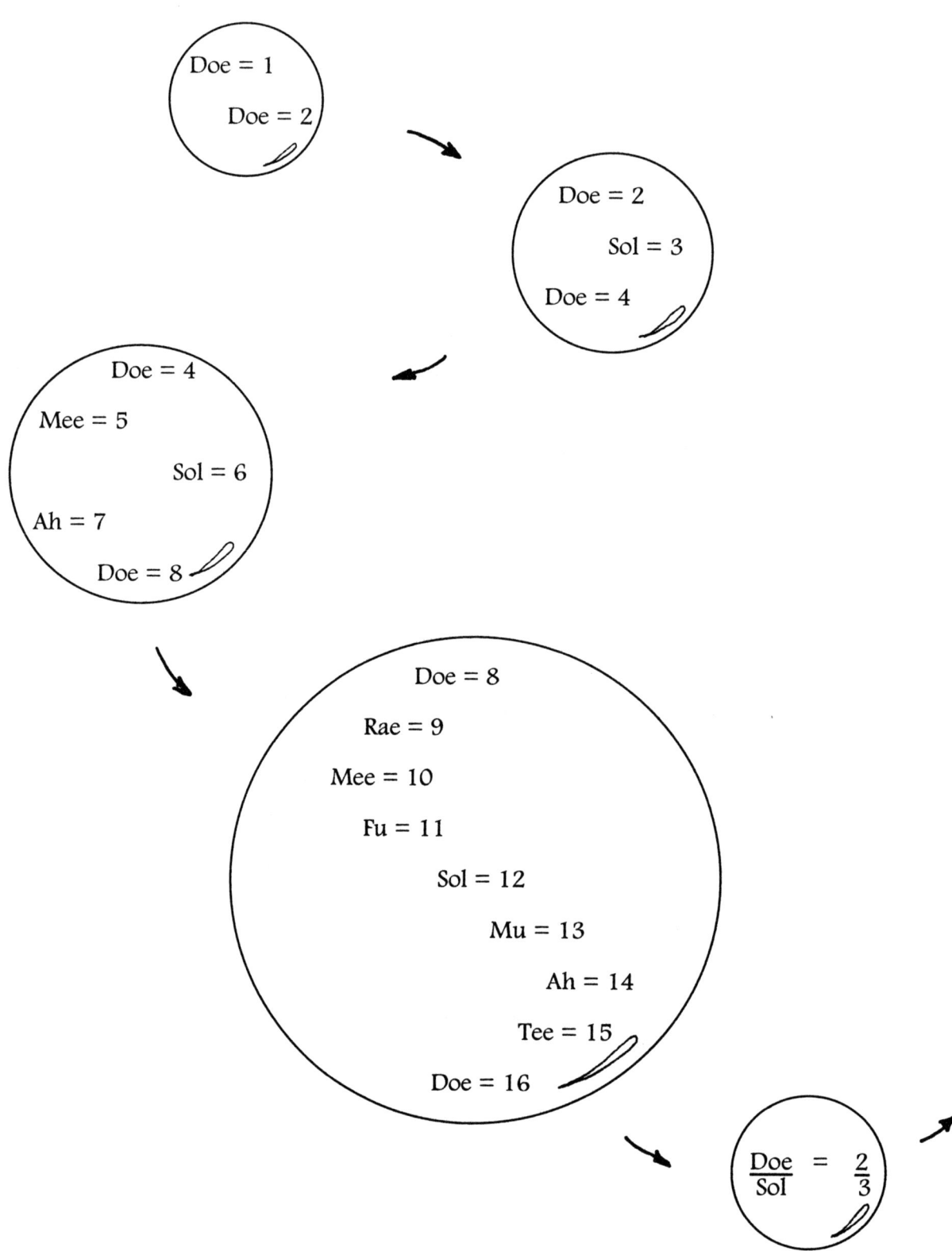

"But what if Ah is dead...?"

Pytag drifted into possibilities.

"What if I create something new, like $\frac{?}{Doe}$

Then, replacing the names with their numbers..."

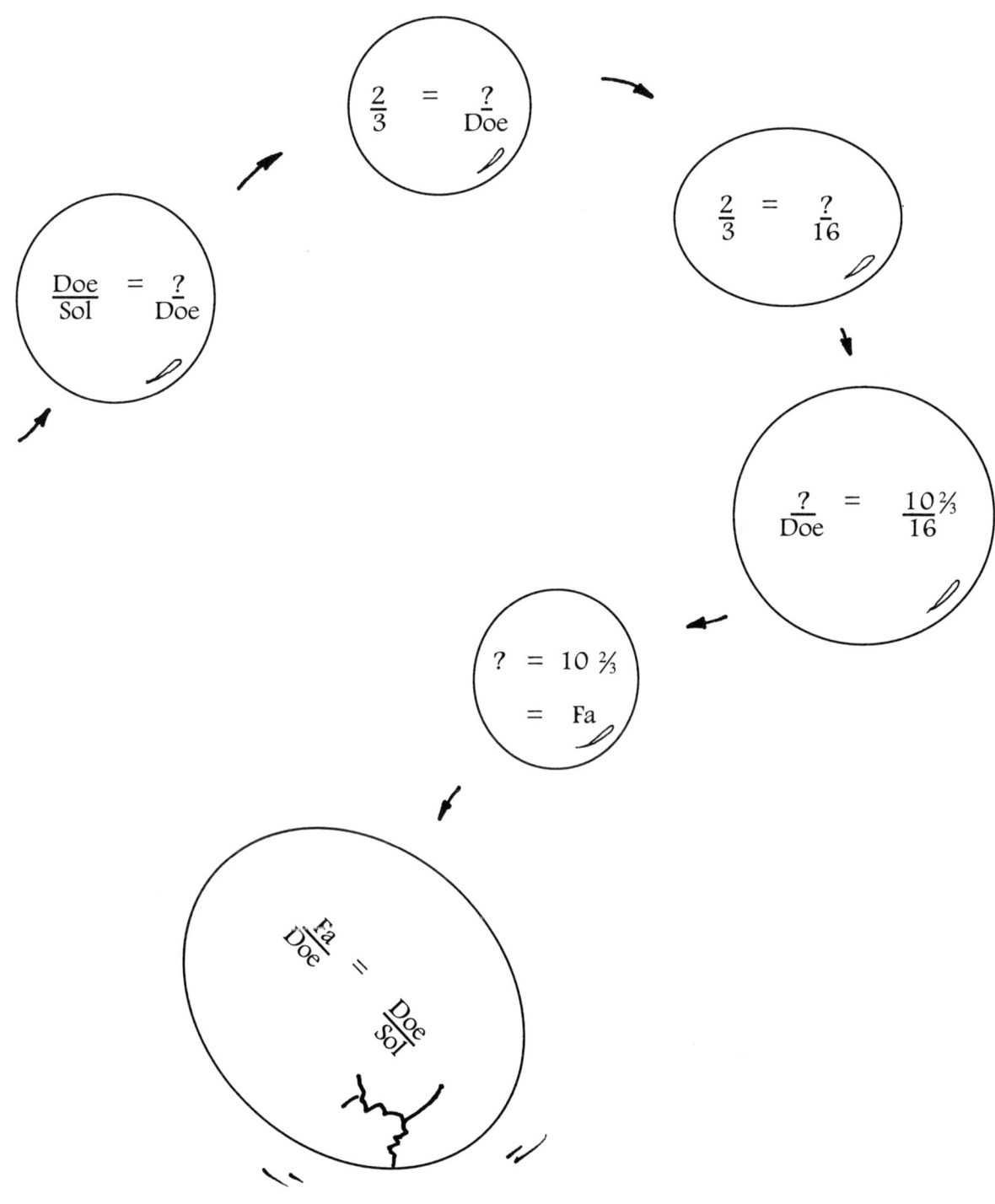

Pytag's mind bubbled on...

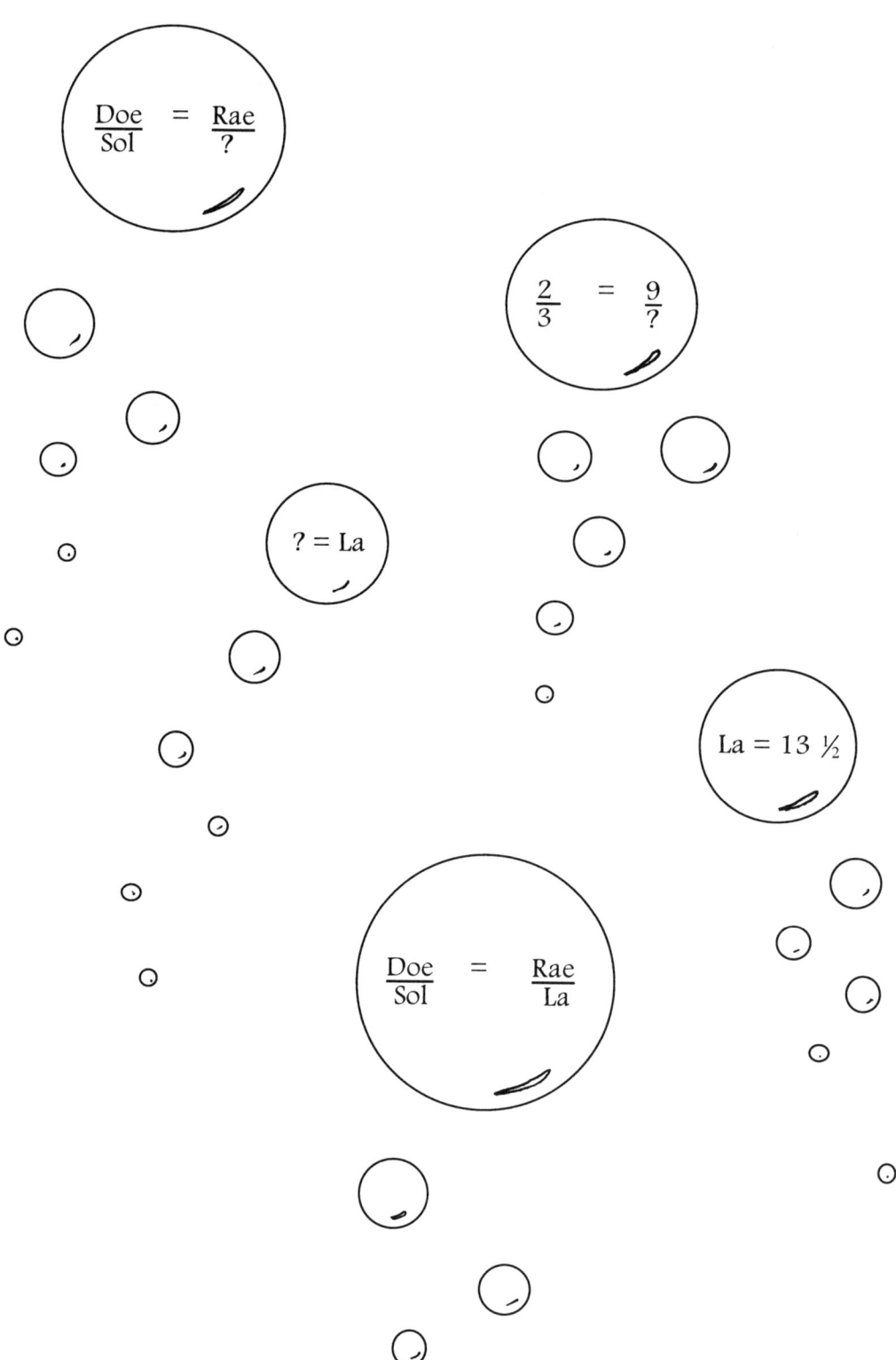

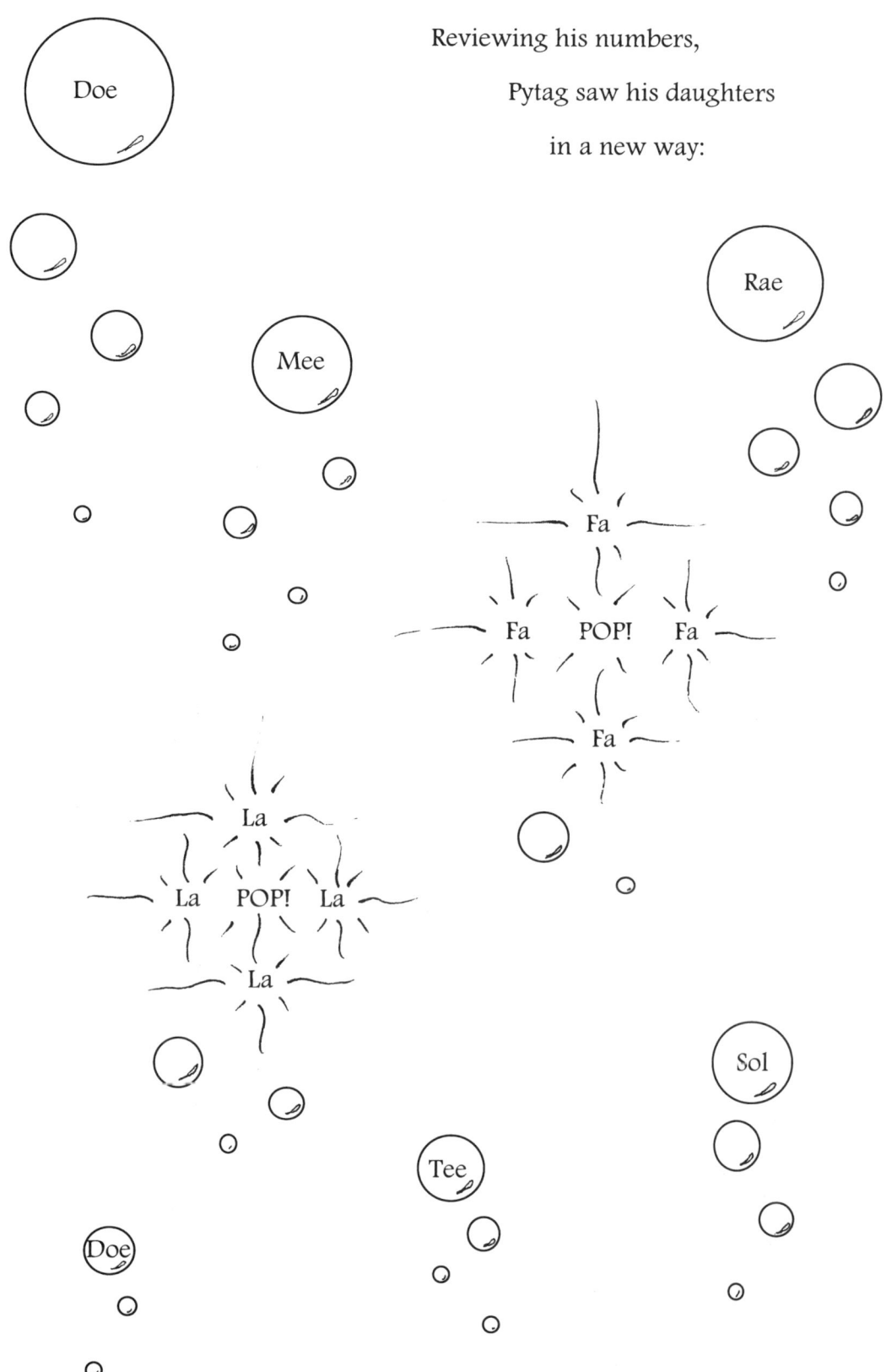

Reviewing his numbers,

Pytag saw his daughters

in a new way:

41

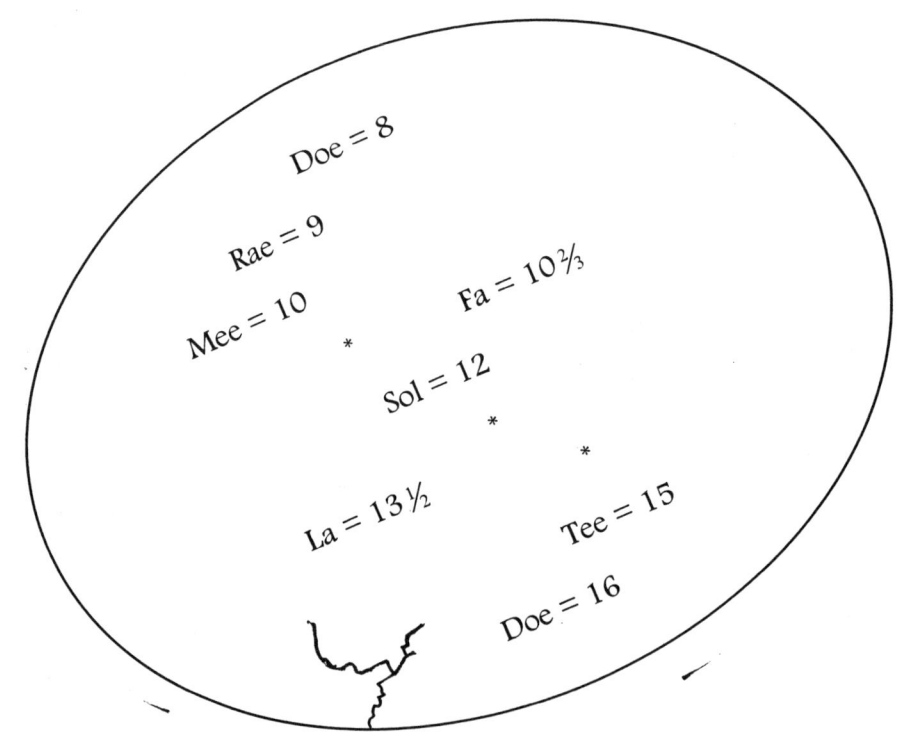

4. THE FAMILY FRAGMENTS

Dream of Tone Berry Jam

Earth begins to hum.
Song feels it in his bones.

Thousands of people stand around him.
They feel earth's great tone...
all hum along.

Doe lifts up her voice & begins to sing.
Rae, Mee, Fu, Sol & Mu join in harmony with her.

Ah is there too.
She joins in with her sweet voice.
The chorus seems complete.

But there is one more girl among them,
their youngest sister,
her voice is even higher than Ah's.
When joining the family chorus
she makes it complete.

Drummers are drumming,
pipers piping,
harpers harping
& dancers dancing.

Birds gather in the trees
& join in the music.

A sound like water pours from the mountains
flowing over a hill where people gather.
Waves wash over walls of a great city,
dissolving stones like blocks of salt
in an all consuming sea.

Great walls tumble down.
A tall white stone castle
crumbles like sand in the rising tide.

People in celebration on the hill
are not bothered by falling walls.
They feast on tacos, tone berries
& jam.

The Rippling Pool

When Song woke up from his dream
he didn't know where he was.

One moment ago he stood on a hill
in a grove of olive trees
with thousands of people
singing, dancing
& eating purple berries.

Now he was lying in a bed
in a room
in a house that Pytag had built
outside of a small village
at the edge of the forest.

He could hear his sisters singing...

Their voices sounded sad.
They were calling their lost family
to come home.

Song remembered:
His mother, father & little sister Ah
had not returned from the forest.

Song got up & walked down the stone steps
to the garden in the courtyard.
He sat down in front of the Rippling Pool,
near his singing sisters.

Morning sun sparkled on the surface.
The voices
created ripples & small waves
that danced in complex patterns
& reflected on the white stone wall
behind the Rippling Pool.

Song watched the wave patterns.
Then his sisters stopped singing.
The Rippling Pool settled.

Watching Reflections of Waves

"Doe, would you sing something for me?"
Song asked his sister kindly.
"Something simple," he added.
Doe responded to her beloved brother's wish.
She began by humming
a low tone that Song could feel.
A single standing wave formed on the Rippling Pool,
reflecting on the white stone wall:

Doe raised her voice
twice as high...
2 waves stood on the water.
& reflected on the wall:

Song was fascinated & watched closely.
Doe went silent.
Song asked Sol to sing a little higher than Doe.
3 waves on the water
formed their reflection on the wall:

Song asked Doe to sing again,
higher than her first & second tones.
She doubled the pitch of her second tone.
4 waves reflected on the wall:

Song asked Mee to sing the next tone higher.
5 waves reflected on the wall:

Song looked invitingly at Sol.
She knew what to sing.
Since she had made 3 waves with her last tone,
this time she doubled her pitch:

A Moment of Silence

Then there was a moment of silence.
A cloud passed in front of the sun.
The water in the pool became still.
No waves reflected on the wall.

"How can we go on singing without Ah?"
 Doe said sadly.

"Where are they?" Mee echoed her concern.

"Something's happened to them, Song. I know it!" said Sol.

"Nothing's happened to them," said Song.
"They just camped out for the night, that's all..."

"Father will protect them," said Fu calmly.

"Where is Momma?" asked Mu.

"Keep singing," Song encouraged.

Waves Moved Gracefully

The sun came out again and sparkled on the Rippling Pool.
Doe began to sing twice as high as her last tone.
8 waves rippled across the pool
dancing in place on the reflecting wall:

Song could see the nature of his sisters' voices
by watching patterns of waves reflected on the wall.
He motioned for Rae to take her turn.
Rae sang a tone higher than Doe.
9 waves danced on the wall:

Mee figured out the pattern.
She made 5 waves with her last tone.
This time she sang twice as high and made 10:

Fu & Seerius were watching.
Song asked if she would help in their experiment,
"Sing a tone for us, Fu."
As she did, 11 waves moved gracefully on the reflecting wall:

Sol was ready for her cue.
She doubled the pitch of her 6 wave tone.
12 waves rippled on the water & reflected on the wall:

Song asked Mu to sing
one tone higher than all the others.
Her voice created 13 graceful waves
on the reflecting wall:

Seerius barked.
Waves on the pool scattered.

A Missing Link

The water calmed.
They felt troubled about their family
who had not returned from the forest.

"We cannot go on singing without Ah," Doe's tone was firm.

"I don't feel complete without her," said Mee.
"We need Ah..."

"They will return at any moment," said Fu.

"I want Momma!" cried Mu.

"We're missing someone else too..."
Song suddenly remembered his dream
as he gazed into the clear, calm pool.

Song spoke to himself,
adding up the numbers of waves:
"7 & 14... That's where Ah should be...
Doe was 1, 2, 4 & 8... That would make her 16
when she sings her next higher tone...
That leaves 15..."

Song spoke again to his sisters:
"There's another
besides Ah...
Somewhere... Sometime...
Soon..."

Song leaned forward
& gazed into the still water of the pool.
He saw his own reflection & thought:

"She is a missing link in the wave chain.
If she & Ah were here
we would be complete."

Song said, "A band!"

"Tone Berries!"

"A band?" Doe asked.

"What kind of band?" asked Rae.

"A family band..." Song replied, "A musical band!"

Mee giggled. "What will we call it?"

"Tone Berries!"
Song remembered the last scene in his dream,
the sweet taste of purple berries
still fresh in his mind.

"Father will not like it..." Fu spoke with a serious tone.
"Tone berries are illegal."

Seerius barked.

"Well, they shouldn't be!" Song argued.
"Why should little purple berries be illegal?"

"Just because Pytag has a berry problem," piped Sol.

"What kind of music will we play?" asked Mu, excited.
"Sweet music!" chirped Song.
Doe smiled.

"Sweet as jam..." Song went on.
They all giggled at their brother's funny ideas.

"Tone berry jam..."
Song's eyes twinkled like stars gazing from the future.
He began to tap out a rhythm on a water jug.
"Let's try a taste..." Song began to drum.

Doe, Rae, Mee, Fu, Sol, & Mu began to sing again.
Fu stepped part-way up the stairs.
Their harmonious melodies blended with Song's drum rhythm.
Waves upon waves moved across the water of the pool.
Sun reflections danced on the white stone wall.

Suddenly Pytag burst into the house & slammed the door.
The children heard him yell:
"Fa!"
The wave patterns on the reflecting wall
shattered.

Spoiled Jam

The children stopped singing.
                         Seerius started barking.
Song rushed into the house to meet the three lost wanderers
      but only Pytag was there.
                                 His ears were red.
       He looked mad.
                    Rummaging hastily through a pile of books,
      Pytag found the Big Book of Numbers
in which his formulas were written.
                                   He opened it to a blank page at the end
             & wrote something down.
      Then he brushed past Song & entered the courtyard.

                              "Fa!" Pytag shouted again.
      He looked at Fu who stood on the stone steps.

       "Fa! Come down here!"
          Pytag pointed with his Big Book.

             "Father..." Fu replied calmly,
          "there is no one here by that name."

                              "Where's Momma?" Mu cried.
      Seerius growled.

          "Where's Ah...?" Doe, Mee & Sol rang out together.

Pytag threw the book toward Fu.
       She lost her balance
                    & tumbled down the stone steps, sitting disoriented
      on the floor at Pytag's feet.

       "Your name is Fa!"
Pytag commanded her.

                "It is?" the dazed child said
          in a very un-Fu-like manner.

The Family Fragments

Doe stood in shock.

Seerius barked & growled at Pytag.
Song held the dog by his collar.

Rae darted out of the courtyard,
gone in a flash.
Mee bolted the door inside her bedroom adjoining the courtyard.
Sol started to run up the stairs
but she stopped when she saw Mu rush to Fu's side, crying;
"Daddy! What've you done?"

"Fu is gone..." Pytag mumbled.

Song was silent.
Doe broke into tears.

Seerius howled.

Mu looked up at Pytag in disbelief.
Streams flowed from innocent eyes.
"Why, daddy?"

"Don't ask why!"
Pytag's ears turned red again
as he proclaimed:
"Your name is La!"

Mu fled
up the stone stairs
one step behind Sol.

Leaving Fu

Pytag followed Mu up the stairs,
leaving Fu on the cold stone floor.
Mu locked herself in her small attic room.
Sol slipped out her own window, down a tree
& through the back yard.

The voice Pytag heard from the attic
was different than the voice of Mu:
strange & high pitched...

"La-la-la-la..."

Pytag looked in Sol's room. She was gone.

Song and Doe helped Fu to her feet & out the door.
Seerius followed them.
Fu opened her eyes.

Doe: "Fu, are you okay?
The color of your eyes has changed...
too... yellow."

"Fa..." Fu mumbled, "Father..."

Pytag burst like a bull out the door,
red eared & raging.

"Run!" Song demanded.

They each ran in a different direction:
Doe to the village, Song for the hills,
but Fu lost her way.
As she ran, Fu repeated over & over,
"Fa... Fa... Father..."
Her voice lowered noticeably.

Seerius followed Song to the edge of the forest.
Pytag ran after him, shouting,
"Son! Come back here!"

Without missing a step, Song called back over his shoulder,
"I'm not your son!"

Song disappeared into the forest.

In the Great City

Fu ran all the way to the Great City
but she found nowhere to sleep
except in the streets.
She found nothing but thrown-out scraps to eat
among unfriendly dogs.

Pytag felt terrible about what he had done.
Everything had fallen apart.

Like a hunter on the trail of a wounded animal
Pytag traveled to the Great City
tracking his run-away daughter.

He found her in despair.
She did not know who she was
or what had happened.

"Fa..." Pytag said to his child.
"I am your father... you can trust me..."

"Fa..."
The frightened girl repeated, "Fa...Father..."

In the city's center
Pytag's old castle stood in cobwebs.
No one had lived there since he had married Joon.

Pytag moved back into the castle with Fa.
Room by room he fixed it up,
dedicating himself
to her.

Fa the Fourth & Lord Pytag

As Fu's body healed
she accepted Pytag's name for her:

"Fa the Fourth".

The people of the Great City welcomed the return
of their hero to his castle.
They began to call him "Lord Pytag".

Then Pytag returned to the small village
for the other children.

Doe agreed to go with him to the city.
She wanted the family to be together,
or what was left of it.
Although Seerius had returned from the forest,
Song had not.

She tried to convince the others to join her.
Sol agreed to go, it being her nature
to follow close behind Doe.

For Mee the decision was not so easy.
She felt lost & alone without Ah to sing with.
"How can a family be together
when some of its members are missing?"
But she followed Doe & Sol anyway,
for without them
she could not sing her favorite harmonies.

Spinning a circle, light on her feet,
Rae said, "It will all be okay.
Let's all go together...wherever..."
taking hands with Doe & Sol.

"La-la-la..."

Mu refused to come down from her attic room.
Her only response to the pleas of her sisters was:
"La-la-la..."

"That's not like Mu," Doe said, confused.

Mee shook her head, "...too La-la for me."

Sol shivered, talking to herself:
"Momma is gone...
Ah is gone...
Song is gone..."

Sol was overwhelmed,
"Fu is gone...
& now Mu has gone away too...
I can't take any more!"

Although lost,
Mu was still their little sister.
They eventually convinced her to come with them.

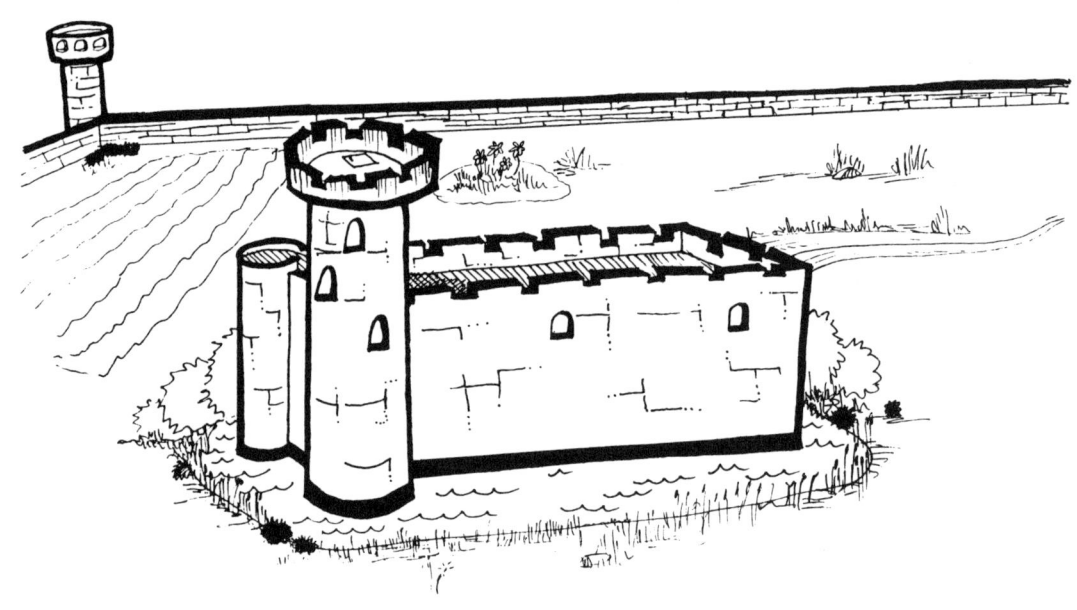

In the High White Tower

Pytag fixed up the high chamber in the white tower of the castle.
When it was fit for a princess, he invited La to move in.

In the isolation of her tower chamber she changed.
She straightened the tight curls in her black hair
& bleached it.

Now silvery locks hung over her shoulders.

"La-la-la..."

Her voice lost touch with the earth.
She painted her moods
in shadowy pictures on the walls
& dreamed of places far away.

She sat before her mirror
for hours at a time
admiring herself,
brushing her hair,
searching for any trace of black roots.

Sometimes, when she was in just the right mood,
she would float down the spiral steps.
She would join her sisters
in the music room
where they practiced lessons
which Pytag prepared for them.
They worked hard at singing together.
It wasn't easy
now that Fu had lowered her voice.

Whenever La entered the room
the mood of the music changed entirely.
Some followed La's voice.
Some, like Doe, felt left out.

Pytag's New Piano

Out of hardwoods
& white stone from the forest
Pytag built a piano
for tuning the voices of his daughters.

The white stones struck tight strings
emanating pleasing sounds.

Pytag used his calculations
for the measurements of each string.
He tuned the pitch
of each of his daughters' voices:

Doe Rae Mee Fa Sol La

But the stone key for La
he singled out
& made her the reference.

"With this one tone
we can tune the whole piano!"
Pytag explained.

Sol knew something was missing
but she wasn't sure what to do.

To Cope

Fa craved her father's attention.
She demanded it.
Pytag responded without hesitation to her every wish
for he still suffered for what he had done to her
in their old home outside the small village
at the edge of the forest.

Fa had developed a fetish for shiny objects.
She loved chrome most of all;
bright polished chrome, sparkling with reflections.
Soon everything imaginable in the castle was chrome covered:
Door knobs & hinges; light stands & chandeliers;
plates & bowls, forks & spoons, cups, pots, pans,
picture frames, window frames, bed frames...

Even Seerius was given a chrome collar.
He tried to shake it off,
but it was firmly attached.

Fa's demand for more & more chrome became so extreme
that it caused concern for her sisters.
But they each learned to cope with it in their own way.
When they could not change her, they let her be.
They tried not to talk about it,
or even think about it.

But now Fa made another request of her father:
"I want the white stones on the new piano
covered with chrome."

Pytag did as she wished.
Fa was impressed
with the sparkling chrome tones.

Changing Leaders

On the piano
  Pytag conducted Doe, Rae, Mee, Fa, Sol & La
    creating new kinds of music.

      "Father, why is Doe always the center of attention?"
        Fa was feeling needy.

            Sol did not wait for Pytag's reply:
          "That's just the way it is!" she said.

         "It's not fair!" Fa complained,
             "I want my turn!"

       Mee also spoke up in Doe's defense:
     "She's your big sister, Fa... Have some respect!"

        But Pytag wanted to be fair,
         "Give her a chance, Doe.
         Try trading roles...
        Doe you sing Sol's part
      & Sol you sing Rae's part..."

        Doe cringed
     doing as her father asked.
  But whenever she sang after Fa,
Doe naturally took back the lead
    & all the other sisters
        followed her.

            Around & around they went
        switching leaders...

Around & around they went.

Blue, Box, Class, Pop & Rock

Pytag became very skilled on his new piano.
He wrote a piece of music called "The Run Around".
His fingers ran around on the chrome stone keys
like Seerius chasing the girls through the castle.

Pytag, his piano & the six girls
entertained the people of the Great City
with new styles of music.

Blue music was sad & slow.
Box music opened a treasure of musical possibilities.
Class music was complicated.

The most popular music was called "Pop".
Everyone liked the simple lyrics
that spoke about everyday events
& familiar feelings.

They called the music with a powerful beat,
"Rock".

It stimulated them
to dance...
       & dance...
             & dance...

The Great Wall of Murlyn

In the castle
in the Great City of Murlyn
the Harmony daughters' lives had changed
from quiet in the village
to excitement in the city.

They were no longer little children;
for in facing the problems & tragedies of life
they grew emotionally strong.

Pytag accepted his role
as the chosen leader of Murlyn.
He enjoyed the respect of elders & nobles
for whom he had built strong houses long ago.

With the elders & nobles,
Pytag devised a project
to involve & unify all the people
scattered about the island:

A wall around the city.

Pytag designed the wall:

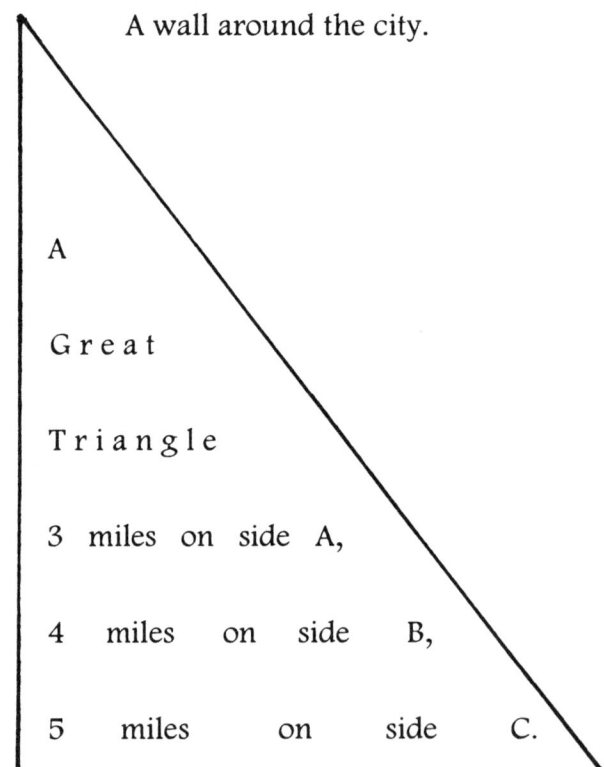

A

Great

Triangle

3 miles on side A,

4 miles on side B,

5 miles on side C.

He invited
the people from
all the small villages
to come and join
the common effort.
There would be
employment for everyone.

Pytag would supervise.

Not-So-Funny

One, two, three years passed
before Song returned to the small village
riding an old white horse.

Sitting behind him was Tee.
She had been born to Joon in the Medicine Village.

Joon had sent Song & Tee
with a message for the family.
But the small village & their home
had been abandoned.
"Everyone's gone to the city?"
Song guessed.

 Riding toward the city, Song said,
"Something not-so-funny is going on here."
He saw the dark outline of a wall.

"What?" Tee had never seen a city
& didn't know what to expect.

"That!" Song pointed to the wall.
"It wasn't there before."

They rode closer
seeing people moving in lines,
carrying mortar & stone,
up & down the wall.

 "Now I know why the Poppers call them 'doings'."

"Why?" asked Tee.

"Human doings," Song explained,
"Always doing, doing, doing...
& hardly ever just being."

Tee giggled.
Her cheeks were purple from eating berries.

"It's not that funny," Song said
as they passed through the gates
of the Great City of Murlyn.

"It's simple!"

Song & Tee found their family in the castle.
Doe ran to embrace her brother.
Seerius almost knocked them over
as he jumped up & licked Song on the face.

Pytag did not look pleased to see Song,
"Who is this girl?" he asked.
"Those are tone berry stains."

"This is Tee," Song announced.
"She is your daughter, Pytag...
Our little sister!"

Tee's purple lips turned up in a smile.
Song noted the expressions
of surprise on his sisters' faces.

Pytag looked confused,
"How could this be?"

"It's simple!" Song explained:
"Joon was with Tee
when you left her in the Medicine Village.
You never returned."

Song's words reached deep.
Pytag's ears turned red.

"They're alive!"

Song looked at Doe, Rae, Mee, Fa, Sol, La & Tee.
Then, with his eyes on Pytag said,
"Ah is alive
somewhere in the wilderness.
I don't know exactly where.
Joon is alive also,
but not fully healed."

Ptyag: "What?"
Everyone but Tee was shocked by Song's words.

Doe: "They're alive!"

Song: "I'm going to search for Ah...
& bring her home.
Joon will be coming home too.
She wants all of us together again.
I dreamed it...
We're going to have a big celebration,
outside, in sunshine, under blue sky,
in fresh air beyond city walls
on the Hill of ..."

"Ah lives!" sang Rae.

"I hate olives!" Fa protested.
She spoke in a low tone that Song did not recognize.

"Maybe you won't fit in," Song snapped, "unless you change."
Then he softened his tone,
"Whoever comes...
just be ready to sing."

Song Questioned

Doe held Tee's purple stained hand & said,
"Let's sing together right now!"
They all went to the music room
& showed Song the piano.

Their brother marveled at the chrome keys.
Then he looked around the room
& noticed chrome on everything!

"This is extreme," Song thought to himself,
but what he said was,
"Cool. How does it work?"

Fa explained:
"Each chrome stone is tuned
to our voices."

"What happened to your voice, Fu?" Song questioned.
"It's lower."

"My name is Fa!" she said impatiently.

La was informed of her brother's arrival.
She floated down the spiral steps
& joined the family in the music room.

Song was shocked when he saw her.
"The piano is tuned to my voice," La boasted.
Song did not recognize her.

"What's happened to you, Mu?" Song asked her.

"La-la-la..."

"Now you know why we call her 'La-la,'" Mee explained.

"Father has taught us a new sound," Fa said proudly.

"You're missing a few voices," Song said.
"But let's hear it..."

Chrome Addicts

They played some Class music for Song
  & showed him many tricks they had learned.
    First Doe set the tone with her low voice.
    Sol joined in behind her.
    Their two voices were the first sounds Song could remember.

  But then Fa took the lead away from Doe.
  Song looked puzzled.
Doe shrugged, then winked at her brother & sang again.
  The music followed her.
    Around & around they went.
    Song tapped his foot in rhythm to avoid dizziness.

      Pytag's fingers ran around on the chrome stones.
      Mee joined in & asked Tee to sing with her.

        When La sang, however,
          everything changed.
        Song lost track of Doe's voice.
      "It shouldn't be this hard to understand."

        He asked:
    "Can you slow it down so I can follow you?"

      They played him some Blue music.
        Song liked the slow beat.
  He picked up a chrome covered pot,
  turned it upside down
& began to tap out the rhythm.

When they were finished
Song looked for a moment
  at the chrome pot on which he drummed
    & said, "Pretty cool...pretty cool...
      You should call yourselves 'The Chrome Addicts'."

    "Chrome Addicts!!" Fa gleamed,
                              "I love it!!!"

5. IN THE FOREST

Song's Quest

Song touched the blue-violet stone
tied around his waist.
"It's time."

"Thanks for everything Pytag,
but I gotta go."

Pytag said nothing.
Rae danced over
& hugged her brother.
"I know you'll find Ah."

Song answered, "That's my goal."

"Good luck," she said.

" Our hearts will be with you," said Mee.

"Hurry back," said Sol.

"I'm going with you, Song," Doe said firmly.

Song's eyes widened with surprise.
"Doe..." Song slowly shook his head,
"I don't know..."

But Doe interrupted,
"Song, I'm going with you."
Doe had made up her mind.

Song raised little Tee up above his head.
They shared eyes.

Seerius barked excitedly,
running in circles.

"Okay, Doe, you're in."

"Take the dog with you,"
Pytag gave his consent
reluctantly.
"& don't mingle with Poppers."

"Why not?"

"Why not?" Song asked.

"I'll tell you why not:"
Pytag grew angry,
"1: They're lazy...
    They refuse to help us build our wall.
 2: They want to do nothing but eat berries
    & act like children.
 3: ..."

Pytag went on about "worthless Poppers"
& "lazy toners"
as Doe, Song & Seerius
walked out the castle door.

"We love you..." Doe called back
from the draw-bridge across the moat.

Riding on the Back of Magic

Song & Doe rode off on the old white horse.
Seerius eagerly ran beside them.

"What's your horse's name?" Doe asked.

"Magic," Song answered.

"And what's this?" Doe asked about the wooden object
tied to the back of the saddle.

"It's a talking drum!"

"Where did you get it?"

"It's kind of a long story, Doe.
Are you sure you want to hear it?"

"Don't be silly, Song.
I want to hear everything!"

"So many things have happened since I left, Doe.
I don't know where to start."

"Start at the beginning.
We have lots of time...
Where did you go when you went into the forest?"

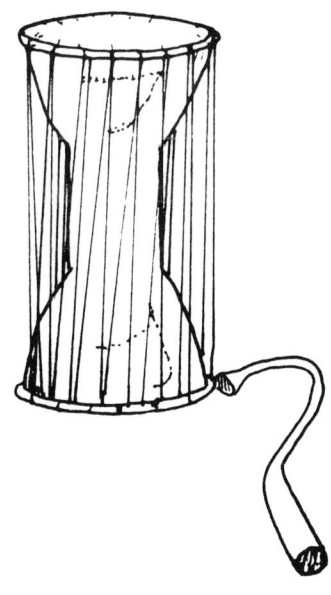

Song in the Forest

"I loved it in the forest," Song began.
"I thought I'd never return.
I don't like to be confined
by any kind of walls."

Song glanced over his shoulder at the Great City.
Doe's eyes followed his gaze.

The bustle of wall construction
still surrounded the city,
long lines of people moving up & down.

"It's kind of weird, isn't it?" Doe acknowledged.
They were soon over the Hill,
leaving the city behind.
Song took a deep breath & sighed.
He gazed at the olive trees around them.

"I considered the forest to be my new home.
Birds, rivers & wind
were my companions.
But I was lonely.

"Then a little coyote began following me,
limping along on a wounded leg.
She looked sad.

"I called her 'Yoti'."

'I'm called...'

"Yoti's pain confused me.
I thought of our family.
I felt responsible
to fix everything.
My dreams were tangled with numbers.
It was too much, Doe...

"I went to the beach
& stayed in a fishing village for a whole year,
swimming, running, working on boats
& helping a friend with a taco stand.

"His name is Gim.
He taught me how to fish.
I could talk about my dreams
& my family.

"Gim urged me to stay. We were best friends.
 But eventually, it was time for me to move on.

"I told him, 'I'm called...away from here.
I don't even know what I'm called to...
I just have to go.'"

Tom

"It was hard to leave that beach, Doe,
but when I went back to the forest
I met someone who helped me;
Tom.

"He's this short, fat, funny guy.
He's got that Sunny Coast dark skin,
lives in a tree house & makes drums...
He gave me this talking drum.

"I drummed with Tom through spring, summer & fall,
learning the way of the forest,
& listening to legends of Murlyn.
Amazing stories, Doe..."

"Tell me some!"

The Great Kite Crash

"Once, not so long ago,
 there was a queen & a king of Murlyn.
 Their names were Omma & Art.

"People flew lots of kites
in those days.

"One Great Kite flew high above all.
 It symbolized well-being.
 Three people kept it flying.

"At that time three brothers were responsible to fly it.
 But one of them crashed the kite,
 tangling the string.
 He was bull-headed & didn't seem to care.
 He walked away, saying:
'That's just the way it is!'

"Everything's been in a tangle ever since.
 The other two brothers
 ran away to the mountains.

"Guess who
 the bull-headed
 kite-crasher was?"

"Who?"
 Doe asked,
 baffled.

"Pytag!"

Not to Worry

Doe's eyes opened wide, "Father?!"

"Pytag is not my father."
Song knew his words sounded strange.

"I don't understand," said Doe.

"Neither did I," admitted Song,
"until Tom explained it to me.

"I was born in the forest.
I never knew my real parents."

Doe looked at Song,
her brown eyes wide in surprise.

"When I told Tom what had happened to our family,
he said, 'Not to worry... Ah is alive
somewhere in the forest.'

"He also told me that Joon lives
in a medicine village,
studying healing arts."

"How does he know all these things?" Doe asked.

"He said all this is written
in a Book of Prophecy."

"A Book of Prophecy?" Doe questioned.

The Prophecy

"The Chord of Life
is Untangled...
A Sound like Water Flows...
Flooding like a Rising Tide...
Waves wash over Walls..."

"Is that the Prophecy?" Doe asked with a little shiver.
"It gives me goose bumps!"

"That's part of it."

"What does it mean?"

"Beats me," Song admitted, "but I've had dreams like that."

"Where did the Prophecy come from?" Doe asked.

"It's written in the Book."

"Is there more to the Prophecy?" Doe was very curious.

"O, yes! The whole Book!
But I don't understand it, yet."

"Tell me more of the Prophecy, Song."

"Hmm..." Song thought.

"Seven Return...
Queen & King Guide People
teaching Peaceful Strength...
The Great Kite Flies..."

Search for Ah...

Doe reached into a colorful, woven bag
for a snack of nuts & dried fruits.

"This is fun!" Doe laughed;
"Tell some more of Tom's stories."

"Tom told me that I was the one
 who will search for Ah...
 I'm to find her
 & bring her home,
 along with the queen, the king
 & Joon.

"When I asked him where I should start, he said;

"'Go to the end first.'

"'The end of what?' I asked.

"'The river,' Tom answered.
 'A dangerous river.'

"'Which dangerous river?'

"'The River of Life!' he said."

"Is that where we're going?" Doe asked.

"Yes. To the ocean...
 where all rivers end."

 Seerius watched with wide eyes.

Earth's Language

"Tom gave me some things for my journey.
 He gave me this talking drum
 & said, 'With this you can speak earth's language...'"

"Earth's language?" Doe questioned;
 "What do you mean?"

"Like pounding stones together.
 You can hear it spoken by mountains
 & big rivers.
 Birds also like to drum..."

"Birds?" Doe questioned. "Drum?"

"Sure! Woodpeckers, grouse, ravens, emus...
 Lots of birds drum!
 Even their melodies have rhythm."

"Okay," Doe was fascinated by Song's perspective.
 "I think I understand what you mean."

"Tom also gave me this:"
Song showed Doe the blue-violet stone
which he kept tied around his waist.

"It's a stone!" Doe said.

'Ho there!'

Doe & Song rode at a steady pace
across the plain.

Song bent forward & patted the gentle horse's strong neck.
Fragrant scents of juniper & sage filled the air.
Seerius barked excitedly at a squirrel in a juniper tree.

"O Seerius!" Song spoke to their big, silly dog. "Relax!"

"Then what happened?" Doe guided Song's attention
 back to the story.

"Well, I was walking through the forest
 playing my talking drum
 when I heard a voice:
 'Ho there!' someone said.
 I looked up at a man in ragged clothes,
 with long, tangled hair.

"He said, 'What were those sounds you were making?
 & what's that thing you have there?'

"'O, this?' I said; 'It's a talking drum...
 I was drumming...' I played for him.

"'My name is Flux,' said the man,
 'Herenow, come up & show that thing to me.'
 He seemed friendly enough.
 'By the way...' Flux added,
 'Did you know there's a coyote following you?'

"'That's Yoti,' I explained."

A Deep Blue Cave

The trail passed beside a pond.
Magic walked right in & started to drink.
Song jumped off the horse into knee deep water
& helped Doe down to dry ground.

"Thanks," Doe said, noticing a yellow feather at her feet.
She picked it up, examined it thoughtfully
& gave it to Song.
"A Yellow-Tailed Fly Catcher.
Don't see these very often!"
He wove the feather into Doe's braided hair.

"So what about this man?" Doe asked,
"Was he a Popper?".
"Ah... Yes..." Song remembered where he was.

"We stood at the entrance of a cave...
Flux examined my talking drum,
tapping on it.
'Will you join us for tacos?'

"'Tacos?' I couldn't believe my ears,
'Did you say tacos?'

"I was starving.
All I had been eating were
a few berries.

"Flux invited me into the cave.
'Who is us?' I asked.

"'My brother & I live here.
We have for many years.
I should warn you,
Will is in one of his moods.
He has his Problem Button on.
He is making tacos right now,
but I'm sure he wouldn't mind if you joined us.'

"We entered the deep blue shadows of the cave.
The tacos smelled great!"

Problem Buttons

"Deep in the blue cave
a small fire glowed.
Before the fire sat a man
with trimmed hair & shaven face.
He gazed into the flames.
Fire reflected in his brilliant blue eyes.
Tacos toasted in a frying pan.

"He had a rough expression on his face
 & sure enough, pinned to his robe was a big button that said:

"'That's Will,' said Flux, chuckling.
 'He has a problem!'

"Will shot us a suspicious glance & said,
'Who is this & what's his problem?'

"'My name is Song,' I answered. 'I don't have a problem.'

"'He has a drum!' Flux said.

"'Okay, you can come in,' Will said,
 as if 'Drum' was the password.
 'But you only think you don't have a problem
 & Flux only thinks he doesn't have a problem,
 but both of you have a problem.'

"Will didn't seem very friendly...
Flux looked hurt.

"Then I noticed Flux also wore a button that said:

"I hadn't seen it when we stood outside."

Doe's large eyes widened with wonder.

'Another Day, Another Taco'

"Will & Flux were opposites,
  yet they were twin brothers!
They argued a lot,
  yet they seemed inseparable.

"Their arguments ended only when one of them
  finally laughed at himself,
  took off his Problem Button
  & set it down.

"We ate the best tacos, Doe!
  Will's motto is:

"'Another Day, Another Taco.'

"Flux says the same thing like a prayer:

"'Give us this Day our Daily Taco.'"

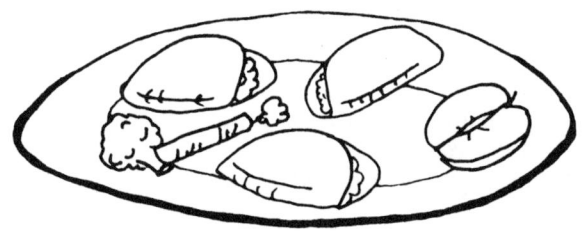

Tangled String

      Song tossed a pebble into the water.
      Circles of ripples
        traveled to the edge
        & reflected back to the center.

Doe & Song sat together quietly,
bare feet soaking in cool water.
He continued:

"After tacos it started all over;
 Flux said something
 & Will put his Problem Button on.

"'What's this problem you two have?
I don't have any problems...'
I told them.

"'We all have problems.' Will stated.

"'Not me!' I was convinced.

"'No family problems?'
 Will stared at me.

"'Well, that's different!' I protested,
 'My family has problems,
  but they're not my problems!'

"'Our problems are each others',' Flux said.
 'Your family's problems are your problems, too,'

"'And all of us have one big problem.' Will said.

"'What's that?' I asked, almost afraid to know.

"They both pointed to a huge pile of tangled string
 covered with cob-webs
 in a shadowy corner of the cave."

Untangling Begins

"Tangled string?
The tangled cord!
'It's in the Prophecy!' I told them.
I thought it meant chord, as in music.

"The Twins looked at each other
& spoke at the same time,
'He knows about the Prophecy?'
Then they looked at me & said,
'You've met Tom?'

"'Yes!' I said.
'Are you the two brothers of Pytag
who crashed the kite?
Are you the two
who disappeared with the tangled string?'

"'We are,' said Will.
'That's us!' added Flux.

"'Then you are my uncles...' I said.
'Except that Pytag's not my father...'
I was confused."

Doe's big brown eyes opened even wider.
"They are my uncles?!"

Song continued:
"The brothers looked puzzled also.

"I told them;
'I have to help you untangle this cord...'
I went to the pile
& started pulling it out from under the cob-webs."

Keep Going

Doe looked up & noticed the shadows lengthening.
Magic had finished drinking & grazed.
Seerius slept under a tree.

"Should we fill our jug here?" Doe asked.

"There's a stream up ahead with better drinking water."
Song stood up.
"Thanks for reminding me.
We'd better keep going
if we're going to get across the desert before dark."

"Desert?"

"The stream is in a deep canyon
 that separates this plain
 from the desert.
 It's a really cool canyon..."

Little Progress

This time Doe took the reins
& Song sat behind her.

"I started pulling apart the pile
 & separating knots into groups.
 But I couldn't find a place to begin.
 How could I untie the first knot without cutting it?

"'Go to the end, Song' Will said, looking over my shoulder.
 'That's what Tom said,' I remembered.
 'Or to the beginning,' added Flux
  looking over my other shoulder.
 'Which is also an end...' added Will.

"I complained:
 'Would you guys leave me alone?
  Please... Let me be!
 I can't work with you looking over my shoulder.'

"I made little progress.
 Soon their advice came over my shoulders again...

 "'Find an end, Song...' said Will.

 "'Or a beginning,' added Flux.

 "'Aaagh!' I cried. 'I can't do this!'

 "'Look, Will,' Flux said.
 'Song's got a Problem Button on!'"

I
Have a
Problem!

Just Knots

At last Song & Doe came
   to the edge of the plain.
 Looking down into a deep,
   colorful canyon,
 they could hear a stream far below.
Beyond the canyon, desert stretched away to ocean.
Waves of dunes hinted
   at rhythms of the sea.

 "They were right, Doe," Song continued.
 "Once I found an end of the string
  I could begin untangling the knots one at a time.

 "I worked at it for days, weeks, months.
     It seemed hopeless.
 There was still a huge pile of knots.
  "I got frustrated... It was such a big job.

 "'Let it be,' Will said, 'for it is not.'
  Flux said, 'Yeah, let them be, Song.
  They're just knots.'

 "I couldn't take anymore.
  It was too much to do alone.
  I was overwhelmed
    & they wouldn't help me
    the way I wanted them to.
     After wintering in the cave with them
     I had to leave.

        "But now I know I have to go back
        & finish what I started.

     "Besides, I miss those tacos."

A Bridge

A trail wound down steep sides of the canyon.
Rainbow bands of colored earth & stone
told ancient stories
of changing land.

"The world's had a colorful history, hasn't it, Doe?"
"It's beautiful!" She looked around with awe.

At the bottom
a small stream tumbled through.
Doe could hardly believe it,
"This little stream carved this huge canyon?!"

"It must have taken a long time," Song mused.

They filled their jug with clear liquid
& watched shallow water rush over river stones.
"Let's build a bridge!" Song suggested on a whim.

"How about over there... by that mellowood tree,"
Doe pointed where Seerius wrestled
with a large, broken-off branch.

Flat stones
were abundant along the stream's edge.
Song lifted one & placed it in the current
a few feet from shore.
Doe began to lift a second stone.
She crouched, lifting with her legs.
Doe placed her stone a few feet beyond Song's.

One stone at a time
they built a foot-bridge
across the stream.

As they worked,
Seerius barked & splashed them with water.

Fun Addicts

Song & Doe rode Magic
   up & out of the canyon.
     Afternoon sun still blazed
as they began to cross the desert.

Doe spoke:
   "So we have two crazy uncles
     living in a cave in the mountains?"

   "Yeah, but they're a good kind of crazy!"
     Song laughed.

   "Are they..."
     Doe hesitated...
       "fanatics?"

   Song thought about the word.
   "Yes, definitely...
     fun-addicts,
     but they just have problems
     like the rest of us."

Peaceful Strength

"Tell me about mother...
Doe reminded Song.

"O," Song remembered. "Sorry...

"Joon studies healing arts
in the Medicine Village
while she heals from her own wounds."

"What happened to her?"

"She was injured by a bear & very nearly died.
But the medicine people are very wise.
They know how to care for the soul
as well as the body.

"Joon was deeply wounded...
the bear wounds were one thing,
but then Pytag never came back for her
& that was the deepest wound.
She's had a hard time.

"When Tee was born
Joon cheered up & began to recover.
She's been studying 'Peaceful Strength'."

The Gift of Magic

"The elders of the medicine people
gave me this horse.
They told me, 'She may be old
but she's healthy.'"

Riding over the top of a dune
Song & Doe watched the orange sun sink
beyond the Great Murlyn Sea.

Seerius howled.

Riding across the desert
to the ocean in silence,
they could hear & feel
the low rumble of waves.

A thin curtain of mist
clouded the setting sun.

"I want to see mom," said Doe suddenly.

"I need to find Ah..." Song responded.

6. IN THE GREEN CHAMBER

To the Rhythm of Waves

In a clearing among palm trees
on a bluff above the sea
Doe & Song built a small shelter,
weaving fronds together.

They gathered coconut husks
& piled them loosely.
With a stick & a strand of leather
Song made a bow & drill.
From a sealed pouch in his waist-belt
he pinched fluffy tinder,
then spun the drill with the bow
until the tinder glowed.

Doe smiled.
Song blew on the delicate flames.

Song & Doe sat close, wrapped in a blanket,
listening to the rhythm of waves
pounding at the shore.

"I love you, Song..."

Seerius curled up beside them
next to the crackling fire.

Doe began to hum,
tuning to the sea's tone.
Song loved these sounds.

Doe's voice resonated
within Song.

A South Current

Morning sky glowed.
Smooth waves rolled into the bay,
 breaking evenly along the curving shore.

Doe & Song rode Magic down as
  Seerius bounded ahead.

      Song dismounted on the sand
        at the water's edge
        & put his hand in,
         singing out,
   "I'm going swimming!"

Doe hopped down & released the reins of Magic.
  The horse grazed on sea oats.

"The water's not too cold," he said.

      "That's strange," Doe thought.
      "How does it stay warm?"

        "A south current..."

Three Dolphins

Song swam out through many breaking waves,
 ducking under the tumbling white-water,
  all the way to the end of the point.

  Alone in a huge green sea,
Song could barely see Doe on the far away shore.

 Bobbing up & down with the swells,
he quieted his breathing
 until his own rhythms became one
 with the rise & fall of the waves.

  Song looked up at the Murlyn Mountains.
   The base of a glacier melted
    near the Fishing Village.
     From the south cliffs of the Great Bay
      a tremendous waterfall plummeted.
      In the mist of cascading water,
       rainbows glowed.
       He had never ventured
       to the top of those falls.

   Three dolphins surfaced
   playing around Song.

  Waves rolled in,
  focused on the point.

  The first wave wedged up
      moving
     over shallow reef.

Ride a Wave

Song was determined,
"I'm going to ride a wave!"

The first peak rolled past without breaking.
He tried for the second one...

He swam quickly
but could not quite catch it.

The third wave crested behind him,
looming up, beginning to break.
He stroked with all his strength,
hands pulling through the water,
propelling him forward...

The wave picks him up...
Gracefully...
Song glides
down the green-blue surface of the water,
his arms extending forward...

Time Slows...

The drop seems endless...

Song arches,
        projecting
    far ahead of the breaking wave,
    one arm forward & the other arm back,
        carving a graceful turn,
        gliding up the wave.

    Down the smooth surface of the water
    Song streaks, both arms at his side...
With a full body arch
    he carves another turn at the bottom
    & again glides up the wave.

    Surfing in smooth arcs
    up & down
    the wave rolls swiftly toward shore.

Dolphins reappear
  in the water around him,
  surfing the same wave.

Song is one of them.

In the Green Chamber

Over shallow water
the green wall steepens, hollows.

The upper edge
turns white with mist.
Wind from the shore blows spray back
like the flowing mane of a wild horse.

Morning sun touches mist,
illuminating it
with rainbows.

The wave curls around Song's body,
embracing him.

An oval eye
of spinning water
opens...

Song is in the green chamber,
in the quiet center of a storm;
water whirling, roaring...

A tremendous sound surrounds him;
a sound of rushing wind & waterfalls,
of rolling thunder
filling him...
carrying him...

...In...

Ocean Sound

Doe was exploring tide pools
when Song emerged from the water.
She had not seen him ride the wave.

"I'm hungry!" Song called out as he approached, dripping.
"Me too!" Doe echoed.

"The Fishing Village is near here."

They walked beside Magic.

"Gim!" Song called to his friend
as he approached the taco stand,
"Good to see you again..."

"Song..."Gim cheered.

"Hey, guess what?" Song could not hide his excitement;
"I caught a wave... body surfing!"

"Awesome, Dood! D'ja get toobed?"

"Ya, man! Into the One!"

Suddenly Gim felt a little jealous
& wanted to change the subject.
"What's that around your waist?"

"O"
Song paused...
"It's a stone."

"It's an Ocean Stone, isn't it?" Gim asked.

"I was told it's a river stone."

"Same thing!" Gim spoke with confidence.
"Around here we call them 'O Stones'.
Our healers use them."

"Hmmm..." Song pondered.
Ocean sound filled their ears.

A Sudden Change of Expression

"Want some tacos?" Gim offered.
"I'll have one!" Doe spoke up.
Song snapped out of his reverie,
"I'll take two."

They each ate a taco
as Gim told fish & surf stories.

"How much do we owe you?" Song asked
after finishing his first taco.

"For you, my good friends...
today... they are free!"

"Are you serious?" said Song.
Seerius barked, surprising Gim.

"Seerius is our dog," Doe explained.
"Don't worry, he's friendly."
Seerius wagged his tail.

"Seriously..." Gim continued
with a cautious eye on the dog,
"Fishing's been good lately...."

With a sudden change of expression
Song said, "I have to go..."

"Where?" Doe asked.

Song wrapped up his other taco for later,
gazing up at the mountains.
"To the blue cave. Up the glacier..."

"We have to go right now?!"
Doe was bewildered.

Song turned to Doe
& took her by the shoulders.
"Doe, I need to go to the mountains... alone.
Can you make it back home?"

"O Song..." Doe took a deep breath.
"Of course I can."

7. RETURN OF SEVEN

A Prayer Arose

Riding alone on Magic
Doe journeyed back across the desert.

Seerius ran in joyous circles around them,
but Doe was sad.
She missed Song already.

A prayer arose from her heart
for his safe return
& she found peace
in her desert crossing.

Face to Face

All is silent.

Doe sees a young deer ready to dash.
Seerius locks eyes with the deer,
ready for a chase,
but Doe raises her hand.
Seerius waits.

At the bridge she & Song had built,
Doe quietly pats Magic on the neck
& dismounts in the shade of the leafy mellowood tree.

The fawn prepares to leap away.
No one moves.
The fawn relaxes.

Stepping on the large fallen branch,
Doe picks a leaf from a low hanging bough.

As Doe places the leaf in her mouth,
the little fawn, a young doe,
watches.

Anxious, but obedient to Doe's will,
Seerius waits.

Birds watch from the mellowood tree.
All attention focuses on this encounter
between young woman & young deer.

On hands & knees
Doe approaches,
pausing.

The little doe steps toward her,
nose wiggling,
legs trembling.

Face to face,
the fawn nibbles
at the mellowood leaf...

Doe to doe,
so close,
never touching.

Up

Up the glacier
Song climbed.
The sea's tone still rumbled within him.
Deep blue crevasses crossed his path.
He zig-zagged around them.

The sun sank lower.
Song made slow progress.
Ocean clouds rolled in,
covering hills below.

Something moved
on the ice field in the distance...

A small animal, limping...

"Yoti!"

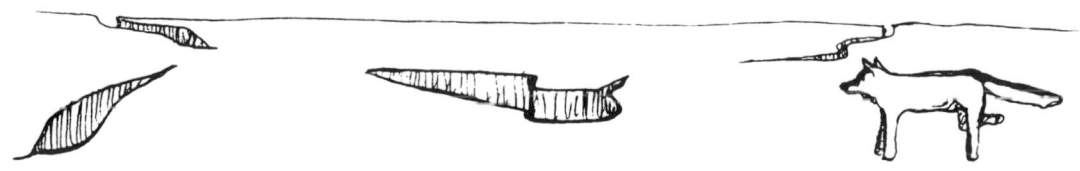

"What to do... What to do?"

Song sounded a greeting on his talking drum.
Yoti limped toward him,
stopping a short distance away.
Clouds rolled in,
above & below...
everything blending together.

"It's a white-out, Yoti!"

Song tried to continue up the slope
but could no longer tell up from down.

Suddenly...
blue shadows loomed one step before him.
Yoti yelped.
Song stopped mid step.
He became aware of a deep chasm;
a sheer cliff of ice,
falling away.

Song stepped back
& sat down abruptly,
his heart pounding.

Yoti whimpered.

Song mumbled;
"What to do? What to do?
It's too dangerous to go on...
If I stay I'll freeze to death...

"What to do...
What to do?"

Song began to drum.

Into Night...

          ...Cold...
              Song sat & drummed.

          Movement warmed hands...
sitting chilled & numbed feet...legs...

              Song stood
          & stepped to his drum beat.
              He warmed.

          Song picked up the rhythm,
       dancing-in-place on the ice.
          Yoti turned in circles,
          howling.

    "This is fun, Yoti!"

   Into night they danced & sang
              until Song tired.
       His stomach growled with hunger.

"Hey," Song remembered, "I have a taco!"
He found it wrapped, mushed in his waist belt.
Song squatted, "Want some taco, Yoti?"

Yoti crept over,
    slowly,
& ate from Song's hand.

       Song stood again
         & continued
           drumming...

     It was freezing cold.
   He concentrated on pace & rhythm,
     thinking of nothing else:

1, 2, 3, step... 1, 2, 3...

Through the long dark night
Song continued this slow, steady beat...

1, 2, 3, step... 1, 2, 3...

Purple Dawn

Fog glowed purple at dawn.
Song thought of Doe, Seerius & Magic,
trusting they were okay.

The illuminated mist
turned red, orange, yellow...
Morning warmed.

Blue sky broke through.
Clouds dissolved
& the sun rose...

Song journeyed on,
up,
around the tangled maze of crevasses
until he reached the top.
Between a notch in the high pass
morning sun shone in his eyes.

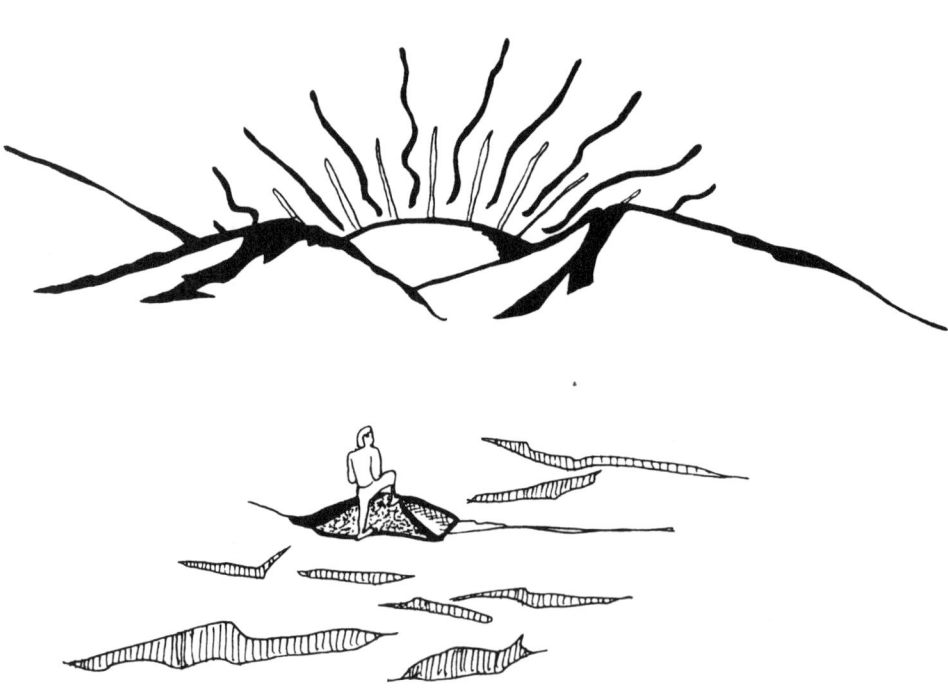

Voices

Song squinted.

Hushed melodies
resonated within him...

Voices...

Voices of the sisters
as children;
before Fu became Fa...
before Mu became La.

Sweet music carried him...

A long forgotten voice
joined the chorus,
"It's Ah..."

Song looked at the blue-violet stone.

The Fall

Song passed easily through the notch.
    Bright morning sun warmed his hands & face.

    Song smiled, traversing above a deep valley.
        Far below, a river roared.

Yoti limped close behind.

    Song could see, on the other side,
            the blue cave.

  Walking...
     Ah's tone
       & the blending voices of his sisters
          carrying him...

  Walking...
    light,
      free of care...

                suddenly
           loose stones
       slipping
     falling
tumbling   Song   Yoti yelps.
   down
     rolling
        into the valley.

  The talking drum bounces away
        pounding:

          "Ba-Ba-Ba-Boom!"

   Echoing down the long river valley...

"Ba-Boom!
    Ba-boom...
      ba-boom..."

"O, well."

Song tumbles through tangles of brush
feeling the stone tear away from his waist.

He lands with a splash!

Song felt no pain.
The drum lay shattered
among piles of dry white bones.

Dazed,
Song looked around.

Water bubbled from springs nearby,
joining, gathering momentum
as a swift flowing stream,
rushing rapidly away
as a roaring river.

Song searched among bones
for his lost stone
but could not find it.

"O, well."

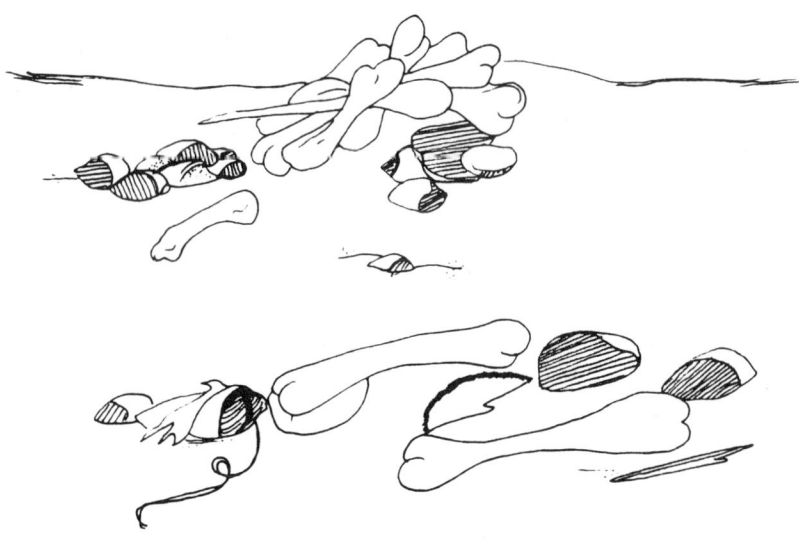

Browser

Nearby,
a young brown bear browsed a berry patch
wiggling its long tail.
Immersed in thick clusters of purple berries,
the bear did not notice Song's noisy entrance.

"Tone berries!"
Song walked toward the bear.

"Boo!"
The bear jumped straight into the air,
feet scrambling but going nowhere.
It landed & tumbled into the stream.

Up the other side
& running a short distance away
the bear suddenly stopped,
breathing heavily,
looking at Song.

Song fell over laughing,
then suddenly thought,
"I wonder where its mother is?"

After a while, feeling safe again,
Song munched some berries.

From the other side of the stream
the young bear watched.

"Hey Browser,"
Song named her.
"Good berries, huh?"

Return to the Blue Cave

Out of the valley Song climbed.
Browser followed.

They approached the cave.
Browser stayed outside sniffing around.
As Song entered, he heard the brothers bickering:

"It's your problem, not my problem," Will said.
"I don't have a problem," argued Flux. "You've got the problem!"
Song saw both of them wearing Problem Buttons.

The twins looked up, surprised, as Song walked in.
"Look Flux..." Will said,
         "It's an Archetypical Mythological Creature!"

"What's the problem, guys?" Song chuckled.

"You know what the problem is!" Will was serious.
Flux explained:
"We've made another mess out of the kite string...
We tried to finish your job & made it worse."

Song went over to the pile of knots & looked.
"Aaagh!" he said. "You guys...
It's as bad as it was before I started!"

"Okay, leave me alone this time..."
Song went to work
carefully examining the pile,
looking for an end of the string.
The brothers watched.
Flux made a suggestion.
Song turned around with a strong look & said,
"Beat it! I know what to do!"
The brothers backed off, humbly.

         "Wowzers!" chirped Flux.

"The kid's on a mission," Will confirmed, laughing.

         Each took off their Problem Buttons
         & set them down.

Drum Addicts

The twins sat opposite each other,
a circle of stones
& a fire between them.

They began tapping sticks together.
Will led a rhythm,
then they traded leads.

Later, while eating tacos, Song spoke,
"That was some nice music
you guys were playing."

Flux: "We call them Log Jams!"
Will: "...or... Log-a-Rhythms."
The brothers burst out laughing,
dribbling taco juices.
A coyote howled somewhere outside.
Song, chuckling: "Drum addicts!"
Flux: "We've been practicing!"

Will: "By the way, where's your drum?"
Song: "It broke. It's gone."
Flux: "Aw... it was such a nice drum."
Song: "Doesn't matter, sticks work fine.
We can make music with anything!"

"Where'd you learn that?" Flux wondered.
"On the glacier," said Song, finishing his taco.
"Purple berries anyone?"
Song offered the brothers some.

"Where did you find tone berries?" Will smiled.
"By the river!"

Flux jumped up, wagging his buns;
"Free..." he Sang.
"Natural..." Will followed.
"A Bun Dance!" They sang in unison.
Will joined in Flux's silly dance.

The twins wagged their buns around the cave, singing,
"Free... Natural... Abundance..."

The deep blue
within the brothers' lonely cave
lightened.

Browser's Dream

Late into night the three friends drummed
on stones, sticks, kettles & pans,
alternating rhythms,
practicing giving up the lead.

Outside the cave Browser dreamed,
little feet churning the air
as if she was running
or swimming.

Browser dreamed this dream repeatedly.
She was in a dangerous river
struggling for life.

Browser flew over rocks & boulders
without touching.
In her mouth she carried two sticks.

It was very important
that she got these sticks to shore.
Somehow, everything depended on it.

She sank under water,
struggling up for air.
She rolled over rapids
& tumbled over waterfalls,
never letting go of the sticks.
She had to get them to shore.
She had to survive.

Browser woke up shaking,
hearing sticks tapping in the cave.

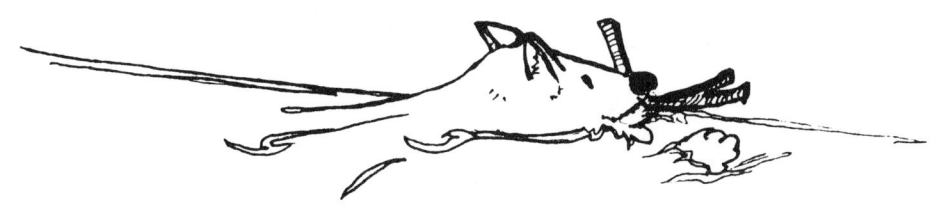

Into Infinity

Song stopped jamming
& drew boxes in the dirt with his stick.
He put numbers in the boxes:

"0... One of these...
1... Eight of these...
2... Sixteen of these...
3... Twenty-four of these...
4... Thirty-two of these..."

4	4	4	4	4	4	4	4	4
4	3	3	3	3	3	3	3	4
4	3	2	2	2	2	2	3	4
4	3	2	1	1	1	2	3	4
4	3	2	1	0	1	2	3	4
4	3	2	1	1	1	2	3	4
4	3	2	2	2	2	2	3	4
4	3	3	3	3	3	3	3	4
4	4	4	4	4	4	4	4	4

"That's it!" he said aloud.
"From the Zero comes the One,
then the many."

Will & Flux could only witness...

"Divide each circle of boxes by 8
& there's my sisters:

1.2..3...4....5.....6......7.......8........

They go on into infinity!"

Will & Flux looked at each other.

"Go, Song... Go!" the brothers cheered him on...

Bricks in the Wall

"Or this way," said Song...

"First ring... Six boxes...
Second ring... Twelve boxes...
Third ring... Eighteen boxes...
Fourth ring... Twenty-four boxes..."

```
          3   3   3   3
        3   2   2   2   3
      3   2   1   1   2   3
    3   2   1   0   1   2   3
      3   2   1   1   2   3
        3   2   2   2   3
          3   3   3   3
```

"Divide it all by 6
& we get, once again...

1.2..3...4....5.....6......7.......8........

into infinity!"

"Ho!" sang Will & Flux in unison.

Song said,
"A wall would vibrate
if a tone were focused on one brick...
It would shake...
possibly crumble..."

The twins stared at each other
in awesome silence.

Singing String

Each day Song untangled the string.
Nothing could distract him,
not even the brothers' frequent arguing.
When Song needed to, he walked in the mountains.
Yoti, the small coyote,
limped along behind.

When Song returned, he'd usually find Browser
sniffing around the cave entrance
looking at him eagerly,
wagging her long tail.

Each night the three drummed
& learned rhythms.
Little by little they understood each other more.
Will & Flux let Song work alone.

Song made progress.

One day Song stretched a length of string
tight between his hand & foot.
With his free hand he plucked the string.
A tone vibrated
& visible waves stood
on the singing string.

Song shortened the section.
Plucking it,
the string sang a higher tone.

Experimenting,
Song found just the right length & tightness
to hear Doe's voice.
He also found string voices
for Mee, Sol & Ah...

Folding the different cord lengths
Song discovered some numbers:

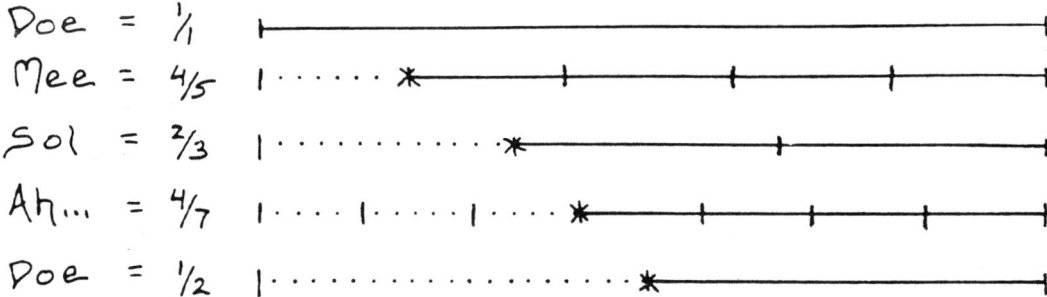

Finishing the Task

Time rolled on...

Piles of knots lay separated into groups.
Meticulously, Song picked at the loose ones.
When he became frustrated with tight tangles
Song let them be,
returning to the task when he had calmed himself.

Finally,
Song pulled the last knot apart
with a great sigh of relief:

"Ah..."
He laid back
& breathed deep.

"At last... It's finished!"

Song closed his eyes & felt dizzy.
Weariness overcame him.
Bubbles floated up before him.

Ah

appeared
in a bubble.

Ah ...
in a
Bubble

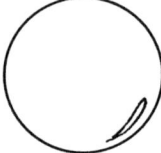

"Song..."
Ah called
in a familiar, high voice.
"It's time!"

"Ah!" Song answered in his thoughts.
"Where are you?"

"I'm here!" Ah Sang.

"Where?"

"By the river... At the end of the river!"

"What river?"

"The River of Life, Song! You know the river...
You've been in it!"

In a flash of insight
Song understood:
The place where he had fallen into
was the beginning
of the River of Life...

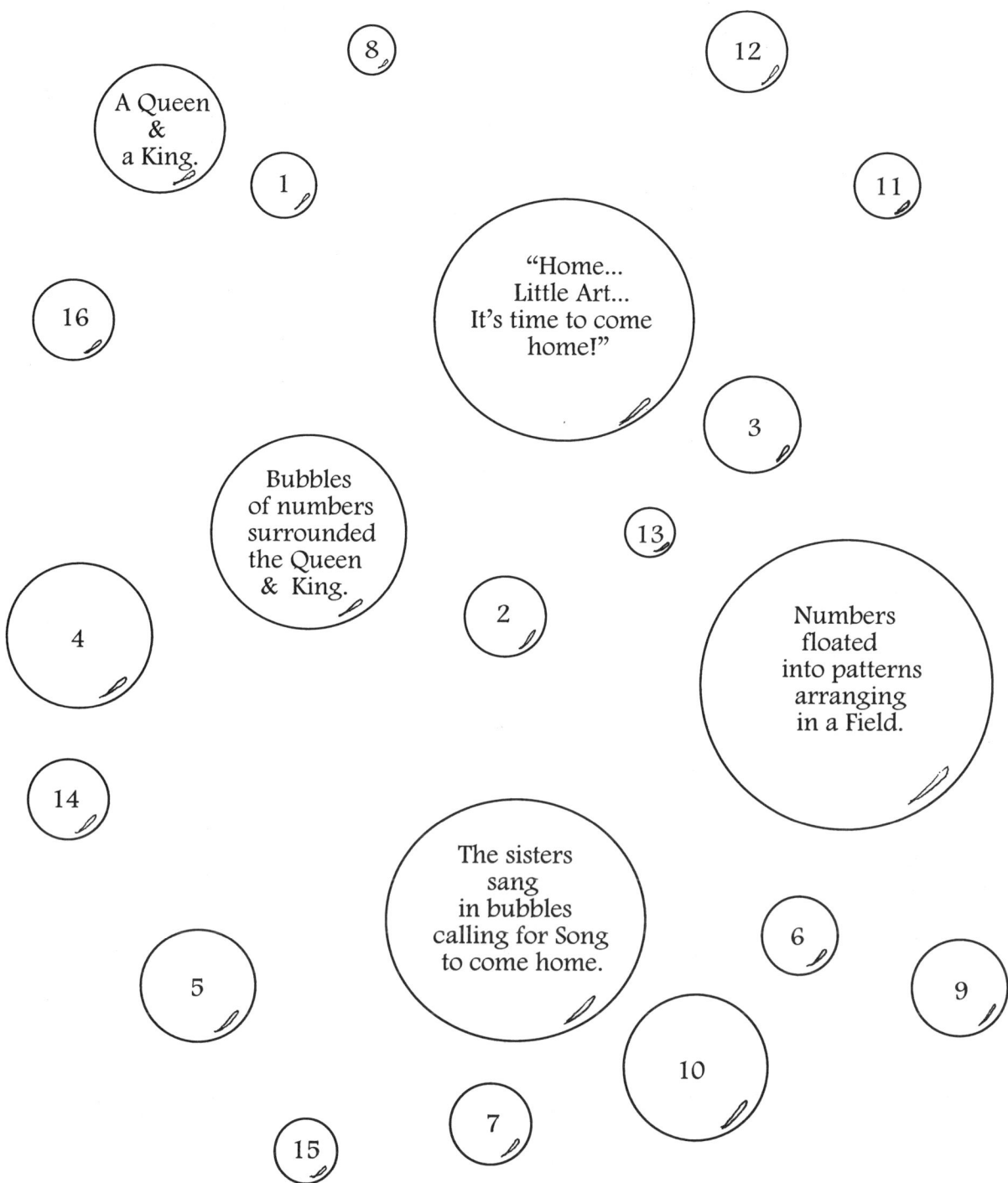

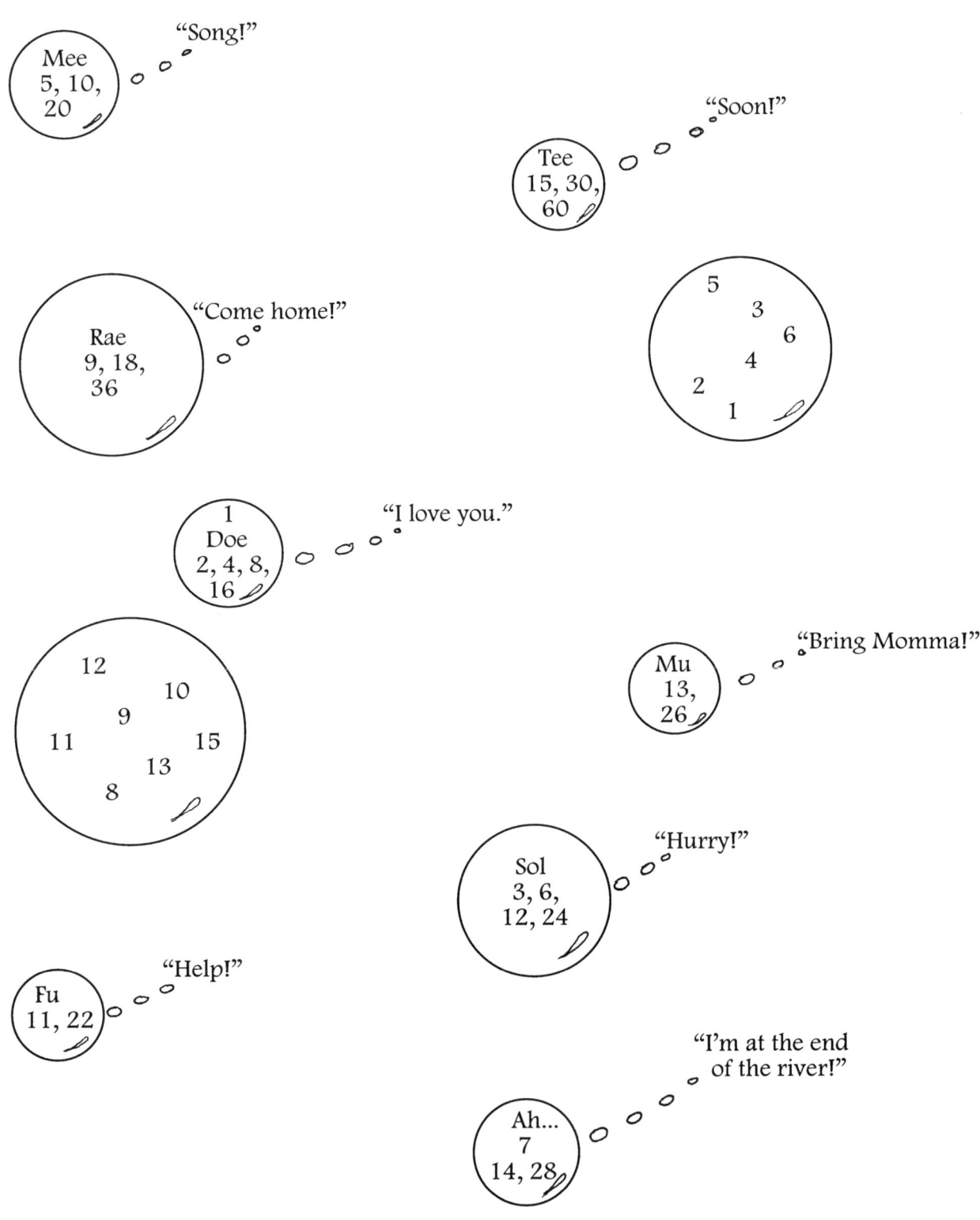

Field of Numbers

Song snapped out of his reverie, springing to his feet.
He began to write on the cave wall with berry juice...

String Lengths

Ones

1/1 . . .	2/2 . . .	4/4 . . .	8/8 . . .	16/16 . . .	32/32 . . .		Doe
			8/9				Rae
		4/5	8/10				Mee
			8/11				Fu
	2/3	4/6	8/12			Sol	
			8/13			Mu	
		4/7	8/14			Ah...	
			8/15			Tee	
1/2 . . .	2/4 . . .	4/8 . . .	8/16 . . .	Doe			
		4/9		Rae			
	2/5	4/10		Mee			
		4/11		Fu			
1/3	2/6	4/12		Sol			
		4/13		Mu			
	2/7	4/14		Ah...			
		4/15		Tee			
1/4 . . .	2/8 . . .	4/16 . . .	Doe				
	2/9		Rae				
1/5	2/10		Mee				
	2/11		Fu				
1/6	2/12		Sol				
	2/13		Mu				
1/7	2/14		Ah...				
	2/15		Tee				
1/8 . . .	2/16 . . .	Doe					

Next Higher Tone

"What
are you doing?"
Will did not like
writing on the walls,
but he let it be,
for Song
was completing his task.

Flux mumbled:
"Purple berry juice
is permanent...
It'll never come off!"

123

Coiling the String

When Song finished writing on the wall
                he began to coil the string.
He wound it on a stick.
          The circular motion made him feel dizzy again.

More bubbles rose up before him:

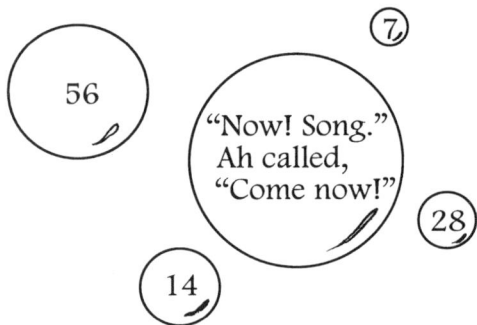

He dropped the coil & walked from the cave.

"Would you guys please finish coiling the string,"
               Song said to the twins as he left.
                     "Meet me in the Medicine Village when you're done..."

Outside,
into the valley
of the River of Life,
Browser gallumphed away ahead of him

Running the River

Browser comically tumbled
  down the valley.

      Song followed,
         leaping
           with long
             strides

           down

          the
          steep
           slope.
Loose gravel flowed beside him
              like rushing water.
    Song began to slide
         but he kept his balance,
               thinking:

                          "Ride it!"

                    The river roared below.

     Browser knew where to go.
       She had traveled this way often.

                        Behind them,
             little Yoti tried to keep up,
        but because of her crippled leg
she was left behind.

Home

Dusk.
Browser & Song heard a tremendous roar of water.
Evening light faded to violet.

In a small garden hidden by wilderness,
three huts nestled in a circle
under a spreading tree.

Three people stood in the soft purple light
at the end of the river
absorbed in the sound of the waterfall.
They watched it pour over the edge,
thick water bending out of sight.

Browser tumbled into the circle,
her long tail wagging.
Song heard laughter
intermingled with the sound of rushing water.

"Where have you been, you silly bear?"
An old man spoke to Browser.

A small girl also spoke to the bear,
but Song only heard sounds of water.

Song watched from the shadows
as the old man & girl patted the bear.
A warm familiar feeling embraced him:

Home.

Welcome

"Ah?"
Song whispered
through the sound of the river's roar.
The small girl glowed
blue-violet
in soft evening light.
Ah smiled.

Sparkles, like friendly stars,
glistened in her eyes.
She looked at her small feet
& caressed the soft earth with her toes.

Behind Song, a woman spoke:
"Welcome home."
He turned around & gazed into warm eyes.

After a long moment,
Song said,
"Hi. I'm Song...
Who are you guys?"

"I am your mother.
My name is Omma."

"Mother?" Song questioned.

"I'm your Father...
My name is Art.
Welcome home.
This is Ah."

Need to Know

"But..." Song replied,
"I don't understand."

Art spoke gently,
"You need to know that Ah
is not really your sister.
You're our child."

Song scratched his head,
"I've heard this story before...
but I still don't understand:
How did Ah get here?
Why did we get separated?
How did everything get so mixed up?"

"Don't worry," Art chuckled,
"We will explain everything.
It's getting dark...
Almost time to light our fire.
First let's go to the river
& take in the net."

The Story

After a dinner of fresh fish,
by the warm light of the evening fire,
Omma & Art told their story.

"Once...
we were queen & king of Murlyn.
The people loved us.
There was peace.
That was long ago
when Murlyn was a small town of simple houses
with leaky roofs.

"Then a young hunter named Pytag
discovered a valuable secret
which made life in Murlyn more comfortable.
The Secret of Roofs was a formula
for strong, dry roofs.
Pytag became a builder,
changing the small town
into a great city.
He even built a castle for us to live in.

"Pytag was a hero to all of us.
We honored him with the responsibility
of flying the Great Kite of Murlyn
which had long been our symbol
of spiritual health & well-being.

"Our legends speak of the importance
of keeping the Great Kite aloft.
But that is an enormous task,
difficult for a young person to do alone.
So we asked the younger twin brothers of Pytag
to be his helpers.
This angered Pytag, who had grown proud & arrogant
after achieving fame.
He became very selfish.
He wanted to do it alone.

"When Pytag showed off
he crashed the kite
& frightened his brothers away.
They fled into the mountains
& have not been seen in the city again."

Song had heard parts of this story before
from Tom.
This time he understood more.

A Gift of Charisma

"In spite of his arrogance
Pytag had a gift of charisma.
When he spoke, people listened.
Whatever he said, they believed.
They wanted him to be their leader.
Pytag wanted people to rule themselves.

"In the confusion that followed
the people didn't feel
they needed a queen & king any longer.
So we left."

"Oooo... That Pytag..."
In the red light of the fire
Song's anger showed.

"Try to soften your temper,"
Omma advised.
"Pytag is not a bad man...
He's just bull-headed."

Art: "He was a great builder."
Omma: "But he forgot to nurture."
Art: "He was a great thinker..."
Omma: "Who forgot to stop thinking."
Art: "He forgot about having fun!"

Omma: "Try not to make the same mistakes..."

Song softened.

As It Should Be

"Okay," Song spoke calmly.
"Enough about Pytag.
Tell me about myself."

Omma spoke:
"We moved into the forest
& there we met Tom.
He invited us to live with him
& he taught us the skills we needed
to survive in the wild.

"Tom is wise.
He told us the Prophecy."

Art continued:
"He told us that a son would be born to us in the forest,
that we would choose to have him raised
& educated in civilization
in order to understand the problems
which endanger the people."

Song: "I've learned about problems!"

Art: "Now you must help solve them."

Song: "Me?"

Omma: "Yes! It is in the Book of Prophecy."

Art: "You have returned."

Omma: "All is as it should be."

Omma & Art's Net

Song gazed at Ah,
glowing in soft light of the evening fire.
She played with Browser in the dancing shadows.

Song: "How did Ah get here?"
Omma: "She was with the bears."
Art: "We traded!"

Song waited for more explanation.
Omma & Art told the story
of Ah & the three bears:

"We are fishers.
We live by the river's abundance.
One day we caught a small bear in our net
which we string across the river.
That bear almost went over the falls
when she got tangled up.
We were lucky to get her out of there alive.
She had two sticks in her mouth
& wouldn't let go of them.
She could barely breathe!

"Through a long, rainy winter
we raised the little she-bear
as our own child.
We missed you.

"In the spring
two other bears wandered by.
A big momma & a smaller he-bear.
Ah was with them.
We looked at Ah & the bears...
Momma bear looked at baby bear & us...
It took a while to figure out
who belonged with who
& it was difficult to convince the little ones
to trade places.
They still go back & forth."

"We've all been going in circles!"
Song felt tired.

"Speaking of going-in-circles," Art said,
"wait till you see my boom-a-rang!
I'll show it to you in the morning."

"Art is still a kid,"
Omma smiled.

The Third Art

Long moments of silence...
gazing into rainbow colored flames of the fire.
The great waterfall's roar
seemed to quiet to a distant rumble.
Small sounds, like crickets & crackling grew louder.
Ah giggled like a trickling stream.

Song sat lost in thought.
Finally, he spoke to Omma,
"People call me Song.
That's what Joon named me.
But, Omma, if you are my real mother,
what's my real name?"

"You are Art, the Third!" Omma answered.
"I am Art, Two," the old man said.
"My father was the first Art!"

Song: "What's our family name?"

Omma: "Gahd!"

Young Art exclaimed:
"Omma Gahd!
But I'm so used to
my name."

Art: "Which name?"

"Song... Harmony."

Art: "As you wish,
you can still be Song."

Ah smiled in soft violet light.

Art's Boom-a-Rang

In the morning, Art woke early.
Gently he shook his son awake.
"Come out to the meadow... beside the river...
The light is perfect!"

Song peered through sleepy eyes
at his father in dim light.
"Your face looks purple," he mumbled.

Art's purple lips drew into a childish smile.
He wiggled purple fingers.
"Hands are purple, too," he giggled.
"I ate tone berries for breakfast!"

Song crawled out of bed & followed his father
out the door.

Art showed Song a boom-a-rang,
"Made it myself!"
He gracefully threw the curved stick.

Wop Wop Wop Wop Wop Wop Wop ...

"See how it comes back around?"

The twirling, flying stick
cut a wide circle through the sunrise colors
of the morning sky.

Song ducked... SMACK!... Art caught it
without taking a step!

"Wow!" Song was wide awake now.
"That's cool! Can I try it?"

"Gently..." Advised the king.

Song threw the stick as hard as he could:

Wop Wop Wop Wop Wop Wop ... Splash!

The boom-a-rang landed in the river,
flowed past the open net
& disappeared over the falls.

"Whoops!" Song shrank.
"I'll make you a new one..."

Art laughed.

Secret of Walking

Song, Omma, Art & Ah
packed a few belongings into woven grass baskets
& slipped them over their shoulders.

Crossing the footbridge over the river,
a log rushed by,
disappearing over the falls.
Art: "Sure glad the net wasn't there for that one!"

They began a long day's journey to the Medicine Village,
in & out of the dangerous river valley.

Ah walked silently, moving swiftly,
gracefully as flowing water.

Song to Art:
"Ah knows the secret of walking."

Art to Song:
"She knows this wilderness better than I do!"

As she walked, Ah sang.
Melodies like water cascading through an ice cave...
Trills like bird-songs rising in thin air...
Sounds different than Song was used to hearing,
yet distantly familiar,
like wind in the mountains...

They paused from time to time,
along the river
to eat berries
& relax...

A Chant Began

Omma, Art, Ah & Song
entered the Medicine Village
mixing among many colorful people gathered there.
The twin brothers, who had just arrived,
noticed them & informed Joon & the people.

News spread among the multitudes
& a chant began:

"Queen Omma! King Art!"

Joon ran to greet Ah & Song.

Queen Omma stepped up to talk,
"The time has come to move..."

King Art continued,
"Let's take this party to town..."

Omma:
"To the Hill of Olives!"

Everyone joined in walking behind the seven:
the Queen & King,
Song & Joon,
Will,
Flux
& Ah.

Songs in Freedom

Animals stayed behind
in the forest.

They were afraid
of the Great City,
the walls
& the people
who had built them.

Music surrounded
& carried the people
forward.

Drums & flutes,
harps & voices
singing

Songs in freedom.

8. TONE BERRY JAM

A great hush blanketed the city.
Silence surrounded the people,
filling hearts.

To some it was long awaited comfort,
rekindling memories of lost dreams.
To others it was disturbing, heavy,
inescapable.

A colorful tide flowed
over the Hill of Olives
toward the city walls.

"Poppers!"
cried sentinels from the watch towers.

Doe, Rae, Mee, Sol & Tee
knew Song had returned from the forest
with their mother
& Ah...

"Ah lives!"
They sang in unison,
leaving the castle.

Doe untethered magic
from the castle stable
& rode out ahead of the others.
Rae dashed after her.
Mee & Sol followed.
Little Tee ran behind them
as fast as her small feet could carry her.
Seerius ran back & forth between them
like a sheep-dog keeping track of his flock.
They all climbed the hill.

Fa started to follow them
but Pytag held her back.
"Stay with me," he said.

"Father!" Fa cried.

One Tone

Doe heard
& felt
earth's voice.

A sound
like rushing water
flowed from the mountains,
surrounding the Hill,
gathering intensity.

Grounding herself,
Doe sang the first low tone.
An aura of purple light glowed around her.

One sound
poured down from the Hill,
washing over the great wall
like waves from an invisible sea,
swirling around the Great City,
rising like an unstoppable tide.

Rumbling...

A stone fell from the watch tower.
Mortar crumbled from the great wall.
Everything shook.

Afternoon sun softened,
lowering
toward the Great Murlyn Mountains.

The Heart Beat

Doe raised her voice
to a higher pitch,
the second wave.

Rae led the Poppers in a dance
celebrating creation,
earth, awakening,
love.

Drums thumped a heart beat,

"Ba-Boom... Ba-Boom..."

Rhythm & Song

Sol joined voices with Doe.

Doe sang her tone twice.
Sol followed with a higher one,
welcoming the return of their queen & king.
Omma & Art perked up their ears.

Poppers formed a procession
carrying crowns of ferns & flowers.
In a joyous ceremony
children placed colorful crowns
on the heads of their noble elders.

Tom led drummers in a circle
around the summit of the Hill,
thumping a slow, steady heart-beat.

Song walked beside Tom,
watching the master's hands
keep time.

Others played interweaving rhythms
with stones & sticks.

Harps, pipes & flutes sounded
rainbows of joyous melodies.

The Kite Flyer

Doe sang again, higher.

The twins unfolded a double kite
made from woven hoops of green willow.

One end was black,
the other white.
They brought it to Song.

"You have earned this honor, Song."
Will handed him
the kite.

"Or should we call you
'Art the Third?'"
Flux asked respectfully.

"Call me Song," he said.
"I haven't changed."

"Okay, Song, fly your kite!"

He uncoiled the string
releasing the kite into wind.
It soared.

Song called to Joon:
"Look,
I'm the kite flyer!"

He was surprised when he saw
that he was not the only one
who flew a kite.

Joon flew one as well,
a purple kite
trailing rainbow colored streamers.
"And so am I..." she sang back to him.

Many other colorful kites
rose to the sky.

The Meaning of Kites

The twins reminded all the kite flyers
about the meaning of kites:

"Wind is like the Great Spirit..."
Will began.
"You can not hold onto it.
You can only flow with it."

"We are like the kite,"
Flux continued.
"Integrated with the wind,
the kite & flyer are one."

"One with my kite?" A child asked,
firmly grasping to the string of a small kite.
The child looked up, uncertain,
watching the kite zip up, down & all around,
seemingly out of control.

"One with the wind!" Flux sang.

"One with all!" Will roared.

The twins danced over to Song,
surprising him with a double bear-hug.

"Hey..." Song squeaked.

Mee joined voices with Doe
calling their sisters together as a family.

From high in her tower chamber,
La could hear drumming & singing.
Looking out the window,
she saw musicians gathered on the Hill.

Drums disturbed her.
She wished they would stop.

"Mu... Sister Mu..."
distant voices sang.
"Come down from your tower..."
They seemed so far away.
La believed she could never go down.

Stones shook in her chamber walls.
Her world was turning upside down.
Confused, she stumbled
through the skies of her imagination.

"Lost sister... Mu...
Come down..."

A corner-stone dislodged from La's tower
& fell to earth.

"Mu... remember...
We have not forgotten you...
Remember, Mu...
We love you..."

La stared
absently
from her tower window.

The Great Trio

Sol combined her voice with Doe & Mee,
forming the great trio of harmony;
a nearly full sound,
familiar to all.

In the city, people heard the powerful chord.
Many chose to flee,
climbing the Hill to join in celebration.

On top, festivities resonated with joy:

King Art juggled eight colored balls.
Queen Omma twirled a hoop around her waist.

Gim arrived & showed kids how to slide down the grassy Hill
on mats made from woven fibers of tone berry bushes.

Will & Flux cooked tacos,
serving everyone.

Kites sailed
in late afternoon breeze.

The Chord of Life

Ah,
drawn to the circle of harmony,
sang effortlessly with
Doe, Mee & Sol.

The great chord swelled,
Doe, Mee Sol, Ah...
filling everyone & everything
with sweet sound.

"Ah lives!"
friends & family sang in unison.
"Olives!"
Fa heard the echo resound
through the music room of the castle
where she sang a sad song.
Pytag played a blue tune on his piano.
Earth shook...
Lights dimmed, flickered & went out.
More of the Great City walls
came tumbling down.

"Abandon the castle!" Pytag commanded.
He fumbled momentarily in a closet
& pulled out an old tattered object.
Castle walls crumbled.
Beams & rafters creaked & cracked.
Fa ran from the castle in front of her father.

Blue sky embraced them.
It seemed like ages since Fa had been outside.
She felt pale, yellow.
A crisp evening breeze raised her spirit.

"Ah..." she sighed,
feeling alive again.

Pytag carried a big torn kite & some tape.
He stopped at the Hill's base
beyond crumbling stone walls
& began to patch pieces together.
"Fu..." Pytag said, "go on up,
join your sisters on the Hill of..."

"Olives!" A forgotten memory surfaced within her:
"Fu loves olives..."
Fu walked up the Hill.

Within You

Doe raised her voice to a new level,
leading a song thanking the Source
for bringing lost sisters back together.

Joon embraced her daughters.
They turned toward the city & sang
for Mu to come down from the high white tower
before it crumbled.

All was dissolving...
castle, city & walls,
washed under waves of sound.

Drums maintained the steady heartbeat from the Hill.
Song joined the drummers, taking a seat beside Tom,
speaking to his teacher:
"I lost it, Tom..."
The master looked at Song's hands. They didn't miss a beat.
"I mean the stone, Tom. The blue-violet stone."

Tom winked & smiled,
"It's okay. Rocks return to their origin.
But now you have the tone, right?"

"The river's tone?"

"Yes...
The River of Life
within you."

Song could hear it.

"That's right... Inside you!"

It's Your Story

Drums thumped on
without breaking rhythm.

Song continued,
"That Book of Prophecy...
Could I see it?"

Tom looked at him for a long moment,
then started laughing...
laughing until he couldn't drum any more.

"This is it!"
Tom laughed...
His round belly bounced.
"You're living it!"

Song stopped drumming.
"What do you mean?"

"*Search for Ah...*
It's your story!"

Song was silent.
Tom picked up the rhythm.
They drummed together.

Young Tee,
with a handful of purple berries,
stood behind them, smiling.

Fu walked to the top of the Hill,
stopping at the circle's edge
to watch.

The sisters saw her glowing
in soft green light
under olive trees.

They ran to greet Fu
& lead her by the hand
into the circle of harmony.

A-Bun-Dance

Sky above the mountains
turned lavender... magenta... red.
Everyone had enough tacos.

Rae hummed her tone, followed by dancers,
weaving around & within
the circle of drums.

Will & Flux joined in.
Song wanted to dance, too.
He traded places with a young Popper girl.
She wanted to drum.

Song joined hands with the twin brothers,
whispering something to them.

Song called everyone's attention to the center of the circle
where the twins comically wiggled their buns.

"Free..." Flux chanted.
"Natural..." Will continued.
"A-Bun-Dance!" The three sang & danced together.

Laughing children joined in...

"Free
          Natural
                    A-Bun-Dance."

Precise Pitches

Orange stretched across the sky.

Doe, Rae & Mee joined hands,
dancing to the circle's center.
Song, Will & Flux wiggled their way out.

The sisters sang melodies
in rhythm with the steady heartbeat of drums.
Singers tuned their voices to the precise pitches
of the three sisters.
Joon held hands with Song.

The dancing, singing circle rotated
above the once great city.

Joon watched walls crumble.
"I'm going down there." she spoke abruptly,
stepping away.

Song would not let go of her hand.
"It's falling apart!"

"Please,
my child's in danger...
I'm going to get Mu..."
Joon started down the Hill.

Song followed, "I'll go with you."
"No." Joon stopped & faced Song.
"This is something I must do alone.
I've been away from my children too long...
This is between mother & daughter.
Your place is here, with the music."

Joon ran down the Hill.

To Be Alone

"Joon..." said Pytag
as she ran toward him.
Joon ran past without pausing.
She was at the bottom of the Hill
before he could finish saying,
"I'm... sorry..."

Joon ran past people abandoning the city.
Pytag turned around,
continuing painfully up the Hill,
carrying his big kite.

Song jogged down to meet him.
"Is that the old Great Kite of Murlyn?"
Song offered to help carry it.

"It used to be..."
Pytag handed it to Song.
"Before I wrecked it."

"Will it fly again?"
Song looked at the tape holding pieces together.

"I don't know," Pytag admitted humbly.
"It will take time to fix properly,
but I'll try..."

"We can launch it from the top of the Hill,"
Song said as he hiked up,
ready to mend his differences with Pytag.
"The wind is perfect!"

"No, not here," Pytag stopped, facing Song.
"I'm going to the mountains.
To be alone for a while
& untangle my thoughts."
Pytag looked back at the rubble of city walls,
"I've made a mess of things down here."

"Where in the mountains will you go?" Song asked.

"To a cave..."

Pytag Departs

Pytag spoke painfully,
"I want to fix the problems I've caused."

Seerius
came romping down the Hill,
sliding & tumbling.

Song laughed at their dog
as he spoke to Pytag,
"Healing takes time...
But don't worry,
everything will be okay.
Just get that kite flying."

"I will!"

"Here..."
Song handed Pytag a small pouch.

"What's this?" Pytag questioned.

"A gift for you..."
Song smiled.
"Open it when you get your kite in the air."

Seerius walked with Pytag around the Hill
on their way to the mountains,
avoiding the celebration.

Fu Finds Her Voice

Song returned to the circle.
Fu stepped into the center
linking hands with Doe, Rae & Mee.

Doe set the tone.

Fu closed her eyes,
watching eight waves ripple
across a pool in her mind...

Rae sang
a pitch higher,
adding one wave:
nine

Mee sang
a pitch higher than Rae,
adding another wave:
ten

Now Fu sang,
adding one more wave:
eleven.

It fit the pattern.
It felt natural.

Olive green
glowed in Fu's heart.

"What a difference!"
Fu smiled,
"Only slightly higher than Fa..."

She sang joyously with her sisters,
"I'm home!"

"You're home!"
Doe, Rae & Mee echoed.

Together, they called Sol to join them.

La Leapt

From the draw-bridge over the moat,
below the high white tower,
Joon called, "Come down, Mu!"

Stones crashed around her.
The once great city walls had crumbled.
The castle was giving way.
The high white tower of La
teetered.

La gazed fearfully from her chamber window.
She vaguely recognized the woman below,
but her thoughts were swimming...
La could not remember.

"Who are you?" La cried.

"I'm your mother! Mu, come down!"

"I can't!" La cried.

"Don't tell me you can't. Get down here!"
Joon leapt out of the way of falling stones.

"La-la-la..." La sang in rebellion.

In the distance, on the Hill,
Sol began to sing with her sisters.
La loved to follow Sol when they sang melodies.
The urge to join them overcame her.

Suddenly the tower window collapsed.
Walls caved in.
La's beloved mirror shattered on her vanity.
She screamed & ran to the spiral stairs,
hesitating...

"Now, Mu!" Joon cried, running for safety,
an avalanche of falling stones
destroying the draw-bridge.

Tower walls crumbled.
La ran down the stairs,
around & around...

La leapt from a tower window
high above ground.

The Beginning of Melody

Sol stopped singing abruptly, feeling moody.
Doe, Rae, Mee & Fu stopped singing.
"Sol, what's wrong?" they asked.

Everyone stopped singing.
The feeling of celebration
changed in an instant.

Everyone looked toward Sol,
confused.
She refused to make a sound.

Song said,
"Sol, talk to me."

"No one will follow me!" Sol blurted out.
"I feel neglected,
you've left me out of your story!"

"No way," Song protested.
"You're the beginning
of melody.

"Without you there would be no story at all."

Berry Stained Fingers

Rae came up with a bright idea:
"Sol, you lead the singing this time."

"Yes!" Doe agreed.
"It will be fun!
Sol, you take the key role..."
Doe passed her castle key to Sol;
"You be Doe!"

"I'll take your part, Sol," Rae said.
"And I'll play Fa!" said Doe in a flash of insight.
"I miss those blue patterns
Fa sang so well."

Sol cheered with all this attention.

"What shall we sing?"
They looked to Song for an idea.
Song drummed his fingers on his cheek.
He laid five long blades of grass on the ground
& five more below with a space in between.
He produced a handful of tone berries.

"The top lines will be for high tones.
The bottom lines will be for low tones.
These berries will be the tones..."

"We can also use our hands."
Song placed his hand beside five blades of grass,
pointing to the notes with berry stained fingers.
"Each finger is like a line,
the thumb & little finger are Doe.
Sol is the center!"

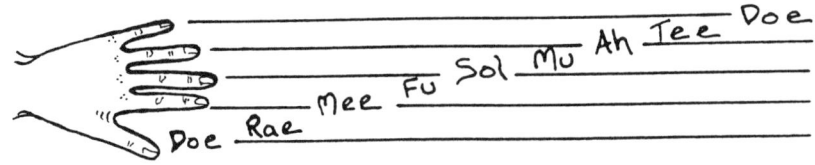

Natural Blues

Sol offered Song the key.
He placed it next to the line
pointing at Sol.

Song:
"Try this,
Sol, play Doe. Sing three tones, then pause one beat.
Doe, take Fa's part... sing three tones & pause.
Rae, you be Sol & do the same.
Then we'll return to you, Sol.
Hold one long tone & we'll start over."

The three sisters sang...

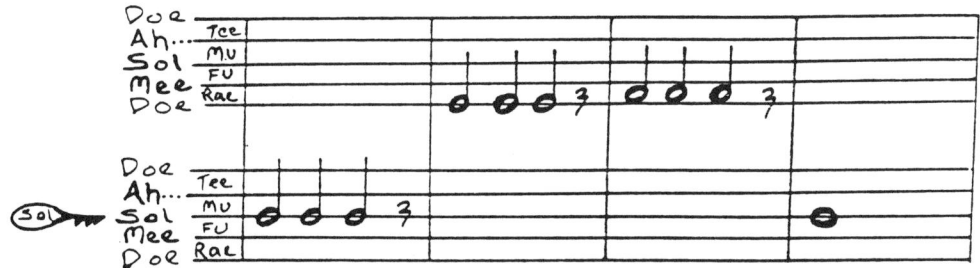

"It's Blue music!" Doe said.
"Just like Fa used to sing!"

With his finger moving through the air,
Song figured:

Sol → Doe → Rae
↓   ↓   ↓
Doe → Fa → Sol

"Natural blues..." Song said, looking up
into deep blue evening sky.

Breaking Free

Splash!

Into the moat La landed in an awkward flop,
sinking...

She envisioned a young girl in a bubble
with tight curls of black hair,
a loving face, a tender heart.

"Mu!" she remembered.

She sank deeper
under water...
More bubbles...

Her sisters were calling her, "Come home..."
Her mother was calling her, "Mu... come home!"
Song was calling her, "Mu..."

She struggled desperately to the surface,
breaking free, drinking air.
Joon was waiting on the other shore.
"Mu!"

Mother & child, reunited, climbed the Hill together,
joining their family.
"O, Mu..." they all sang, hugging & kissing her,
wiping away her tears.
"Welcome home!"

Doe, Rae, Mee, Fu & Sol
sang a rising melody.
Mu followed naturally.

Healers Teaching

Two old people rode through the crowd on their horses.
Joon approached them.

"Greetings."
Joon smiled with love
into their old weathered faces.

"All eight of my daughters are here now:
Doe, Rae, Mee, Fu, Sol, Mu, Ah & Tee."

Woman elder:
"Now is the time. We will speak with them.
We request the presence of Song, also.
Song knows the secret of numbers
about which we will speak.
Song now understands the old ways
& will teach them in a new way."

Joon introduced the elders to her daughters,
"These are the healers."
Song stood silently at their side.
"I owe my life to these two.
They healed my wounds, nurtured me back to health
& taught me peaceful strength."

The elder woman spoke:
"At the beginning of time
the Void awakens & sings out
creation."

The elder man added:
"Flesh & bones resonate the Chord of Life."

The elder woman continued:
"Healing begins
with spirals & circles of sound
reshaping the misshapen world.
The mind also heals
in harmony with this great chord
& the original Void."

The elder man finished:
"Doe, Mee, Sol & Ah...
you four lead healing melodies.
This is the foundation of peaceful strength."

"Mellowood"

The sisters went to help
tune musical instruments.

Song relaxed under an olive tree.
Gim snuck up on him.
"Yo!" he attacked with a bear hug.
"Dood!" They rolled around, laughing.

"I went to the cave, Song..." Gim puffed.
"I saw your numbers on the wall..."

The two friends sat to catch their breath.
"How did you find the cave?" Song wondered.

"I followed a coyote...
I made something for you."
Gim produced a wooden box
from behind the tree.

Nine narrow pieces of wood rested beside each other,
suspended over the box on sturdy twine.

"I shaped them myself!" Gim boasted.
"And I carved your sisters' names
into each one. Check it out:"

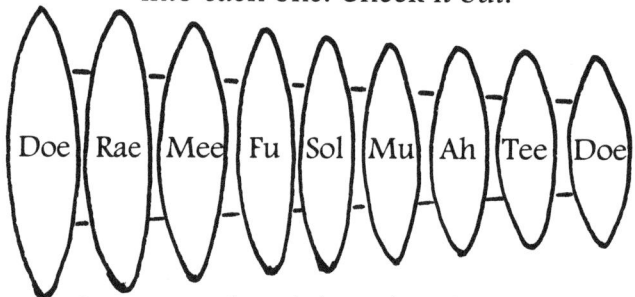

Song tapped each board with a finger.
"What kind of wood is this?"

"Mellowood."

"Doe to Doe"

"Where'd you find a mellowood tree?"
Song was curious,
"I only know of one."

Gim: "By a stream
between the high plain
& the desert.
Beside a stepping-stone bridge.
I saw some familiar tracks there.
They looked like Seerius, Magic & Doe's."

"Two Does."
Gim's perceptive eyes narrowed.
"One was a little deer.
They had a close encounter,
face to face.
Under the mellowood tree lay a branch
with Doe's footprint on it."

Gim's sea blue eyes shimmered.
"I carried it
all the way to the cave."

"Wow..." Song tapped each board,
marveling at their tones,
"Doe to Doe."

"My Rimba"

"You designed this, Gim?" Song asked.
"What do you call it?"

"My Rimba," Gim smiled.
"I figured out your Field of Numbers, too.
The tone of Doe's voice stayed in my head
after you two had left the beach.

"I cut some cord from the big spool in the cave
& stretched it
to sound Doe's tone.
While I plucked each tone,
using your numbers,
I tuned my Rimba!"

Song: "How'd ya do that?"

Gim: "Thin the board to lower its tone.
Shorten the board to raise its tone.
C'mon, play it, Song!"

Gim offered two thumpers.

"Just Fu'en around"

On the ends of two sticks
Gim had wadded balls of dried goo.

With one of these thumpers, Song began.
He started with Fu, and counted out beats...

One   Two   Three & Four &
One   Two   Three & Four

Song varied the tones to the beats:

Fu   Fu   Fu Sol Mu Sol
Mee Mee Mu Sol Fu ...

"Wait,"
Song smoothed out an area of dirt
& with his thumper wrote:

Song began again, with both thumpers,
playing the tones on the beats,
moving into a flowing jam.

He played around Fu,
then climbed up to play around Doe,
then scaled down to play around the lower Doe.

Song climbed up high, playing fast.
He dropped down low & played slow,
then back to play around Fu.

Song stopped jamming.
"Just Fu'en around, bro."

Prelude to the Question

In soft evening light
Queen Omma & King Art had heard Song's melodies.
They came closer to listen
& saw animals gathered around.

Song noticed Art watching him
& stopped playing.
"Excuse me, Gim.
I need to talk to my dad."

Gim started playing Song's melody,
"Just Fu'en Around".

Song walked over & stood before his parents.

"Can I speak with you, dad?
Alone..."

They walked closer to the circle of music.
Song directed Art's attention toward Doe.
She again led her sisters & other singers
in a unified chorus.

"I want to marry her, dad."

Art smiled.
"Son, you have my blessings.
If she accepts your offer she will one day be a fine queen;
strong & peaceful like your mother."

"How do I..."
Song stuttered,
"What should I say?"

"You are Song,"
Art laughed.
"Words come naturally."

"Do you think she'll say yes?"

"That..." Art grinned, "I wouldn't know."

Tone Berry Jam

Evening light turned violet...
twilight...
night.

Song stood quietly,
pondering his father's words.

Art:
"I must share a secret with you.
The Prophecy says;

'A New Art will be King.
A Queen, born into a Family of Harmony
with Seven Sisters,
Leads all who Listen to the Music of Life.
She will have Song in her Heart.'

"That sounds to me like
you & Doe,"
the king winked & smiled.

Song remained quiet.

Art:
"Hey, let's make boom-a-rangs tomorrow.
Sound good, Song?"

Drums mellowed, dancing slowed.
Around the fire, Poppers roasted tallgrass seeds,
singing quiet lullabies.

A woven grass basket full of tone berries
passed around.
People munched, giggling.

Purple lips pressed purple kisses
on cheeks & arms.
Some painted purple patterns on their faces.

Tone berry jam
flowed.

9. THE STORIES IN THE STARS

Three Bears

Late that night under bright stars
around the fire
Ah began to hum a high tone,
warming her voice.

"In the night sky,
as on earth, there are animals
& people...

"This is a story of three bears:
Momma bear, brother bear & baby bear..."

Eyes in the shadows of olive trees
blinked & sparkled
reflecting fire light.

"Momma's name is Urr.
Urr's a great big bear!"
Ah pointed to the Big Dipper.

"Brother bear's name is Bootes.
He has long legs & runs very fast."
Ah pointed to stars following Urr.

"Baby bear's name is Browser,"
Ah pointed to the Little Dipper.

"Between momma & baby bear
a river flows from mountains in the sky,
toward stars called The King.
There it pours over a cliff
into a bay far below..."

Her Story

"Baby bear fell in the river
& was carried away toward a waterfall,
but she got tangled in the net of a fisherman who lived there.
His name is Art. He's the King.
He is beside Queen Omma."

Around the crackling fire
people gazed with wonder into a wilderness of stars.
They had heard legends about the night sky,
but not this one.

"I was playing by the river
when Browser fell in.

"Momma came running...
In confusion Urr mistook me for her baby,
snatching me up & running into the forest.

"I slept between her paws all winter
& played with Bootes when we awoke.
We ran together through the forest.

"I believed I was a bear
until we came upon the fisher people & Browser.
The bear thought she was their child.

"When I discovered I was people, like the fishers,
& that Browser was momma bear's lost baby,
we switched places!"

In Violet Light

Tee sat next to Ah.
Poppers gathered around the fire,
passing berries, popping tallgrass seeds,
listening, giggling.

Flames flickered & danced,
snapping
with Ah's story.

Tee hummed along,
her voice a tone higher than Ah's.

The two youngest sisters
smiled sweetly,
feeling at home beside each other.

Faces glowed
in violet light.

Purple lips smiled.

The Stories in the Stars

"Ah..."
A young Popper girl bounced up & down,
"Tell us some more about the stories in the stars!"

Ah smiled & continued.

"Stars are our teachers & friends.
They sing
stories of long ago
& stories of what will be.

"They sing of the great circle:
Everything goes around
& returns...

"My favorite story is of a woman
who holds an unseen cord to a great bird of the spirit."
Ah pointed to Orion & Gemini.

"We call this woman:
'The One Who Flies
with the Spirit.'"

"That's a beautiful story, Ah,"
said the Popper girl.

"O, but there's a sad part in this story."
Ah paused, pointing to stars
between the woman & her daughters.
"There's a bull who breaks up the family
leaving the children
to fix it."

Who Flies the Great Kite

In a small, quiet clearing surrounded by olive trees,
away from the crowded camp fire
Doe & Song sat together in silence,
gazing at twinkling stars.

A soft fire in their hearts
warmed them from within.
They felt at home with each other,
at peace.

Song gazed at Orion.

"You know..." Song mused,
"I don't see a hunter killing an animal...
I see a kite flyer!

"Can you see the double kite?
It's huge!
Can you see the twin stars way up there?"

Song leaped to his feet pretending to be Orion,
looking up,
holding a great cord.

"I'm the kite flyer!"

177

A Woman

"O Song," Doe giggled,
"Your brainstring is tangled.
The kite flyer is a woman!
She holds the cord.
Her feet are on the ground.

"It's time you come down to earth, Song.
You're like a runaway kite,
away you go..."

Doe caught him by surprise at the ankles.
Song wobbled & plopped down beside her.
"Do you know about the River of Life?"
Doe asked.

"It's in the mountains," Song said, puzzled.
"I've followed it from the beginning, why?"

Doe pointed to a long stream of winking lights
flowing below Orion.
"The river flows from the woman."

The River of Life

"Where?" Song squinted.

"It's a little nebulous where it begins," Doe explained.

"There are three stars under her belt.
The River of Life begins there & flows down
behind the trees
connecting her with earth."

"I see a big dog... Seerius!"
Song interrupted,
"& there's Yoti
& there's Magic!

"O, there's Pytag,
the Bull-Head
& the Sisters."

"There you go, drifting away again, Song."
Doe frowned.

"I'm sorry, Doe..." Song jittered.

Song: "Ummm...

"D...D...D...Doe...?"

(awkward silence)

What Is Important?

Early morning.

Pytag sits with Seerius
outside the blue cave
watching the sunrise.

The river
in the valley far below
rumbles.

Pytag uncoils the great spool of string
& releases his old kite
into wind.

It soars!

"What is important?"
Pytag questions.

He shakes his head,
"I belicved I was The Kite Flier
rather than a kite flier.
It doesn't matter who flies the kite.

"What is important
is integrity."

Pytag closes his eyes
& sings an old familiar chord
with new feeling,

"Doe

        Mee

                Sol

                        Ah..."

Three Berries

From his pocket
Pytag pulls out Song's little pouch
& opens it:
three purple berries inside.

"Tone berries?"
After a moment of hesitation
he places one on his tongue,
rolling it into his mouth...
"Oooo..."

A smile
grows on his face.
After the second berry,
"Mmmm..."

Pytag thinks about Song's writing on the wall,
he thinks about his daughters,
he thinks about Joon
& feels good.

Pytag watches the kite soar
high among moving clouds.
He takes a deep breath,
releasing everything to the wind.

Giggling,
Pytag reveals to his dog,
"I'm having fun!"

Seerius howls.

A Sound

Smiling,
Pytag places the third berry
in his mouth.

Juice bursts on his taste buds,
spurting from his lips,
dribbling purple down his chin.

A sound rose,

"Ah..."

The End...

Theory

"Aristotle says in the book of secrets
that communicating too many arcana of nature and art
breaks a celestial seal...
Which does not mean that secrets must not be revealed,
but that the learned must decide when and how."

The Name of the Rose by Umberto Eco

Contents

Harmonic Overtones

"...the equations of waves can describe a swinging pendulum;
a vibrating drum head; flapping butterfly wings;
cycling hands of a clock; beating hearts;
planets orbiting the sun,
or electrons circling an atom's nucleus;
the thrust and return of an auto engine's pistons;
the spacing of atoms in a crystal; the rise and fall of the tide; the recurrence of seasons..."

Shufflebrain by Paul Pietsch

When a stretched string is plucked
a pure tone is difficult to achieve.
What occurs is a sequence of "overtones".
The fundamental tone vibrates;
Doe...
A single wave.

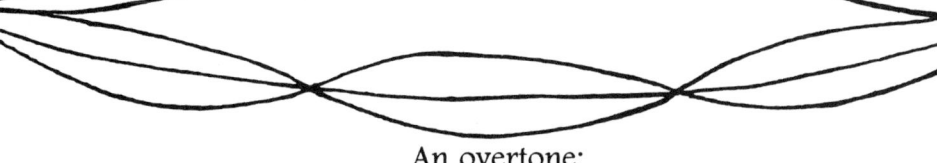

Then,
two waves appear, Doe again,
the first overtone, the second harmonic,
twice as fast as one.

And,
three waves, Sol,
three times the frequency as one.

Four waves, five waves,
higher in frequency,
shorter in wavelength.

Six, seven, eight...
less intense...
less energy...
fading into infinity.

An overtone:
three waves riding one.

Open String Harmonics

1. Fundamental: Doe

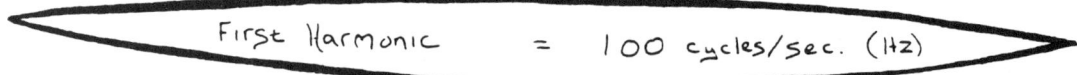

2. Doe

3. Sol

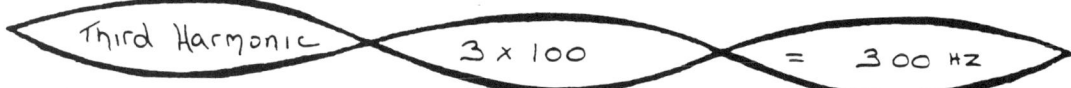

4. Doe

5. Mee

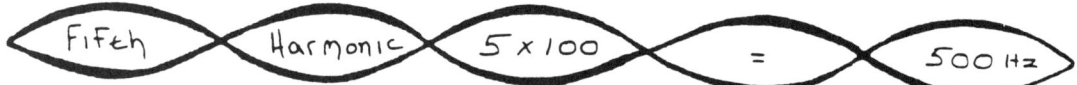

6. Sol

7. Ah

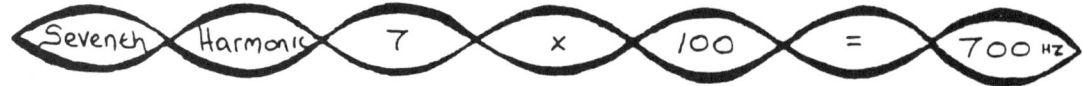

Notice: Each harmonic is a whole number multiple of the fundamental tone.
(See number-correlated notes opposite.)

Understanding Open String Harmonics

Each of the following numbers relates to the wave forms on the previous page.

1. 100 cycles per second (hertz or Hz) was arbitrarily chosen to illustrate the mathematical simplicity of harmonic principles. In tuning musical instruments we used 32.75 Hz as the fundamental tone. Multiplying by integers 8 through 15 yields an eight tone scale beginning with Doe at 262 Hz (middle C).

2. Half the string length and double the frequency (octave law) of the fundamental tone produces the same "pitch class" ("Doe" or "C") through each octave.

3. Each odd numbered harmonic introduces a new pitch class; a tone with new characteristics and a new name. "Sol" enters here with 3 waves and 3 times the frequency of the fundamental.

4. "Fourth harmonic" is physics language and not to be confused with the popular term "harmonic fourth". The (even numbered) harmonic can be transformed with the octave law to the Fundamental Tone. It is therefore in the same pitch class, "Doe".

5. The fifth harmonic, "Mce" is not to be confused with the popular term, "harmonic fifth" which is "Sol".

6. The sixth harmonic, "Sol" (one Octave higher than 3) has a frequency six times that of the fundamental.

7. "Ah" is the name we have chosen for the seventh wave in the harmonic series. This tone is unnamed and not used in Western music scales.

The Sisters

The following is our proposed 8 tone musical scale:

Each of these overtones are created naturally

out of the fundamental tone (1)

precisely at these whole number intervals.

Notice: Between each tone

is an identical number of cycles per second (Hz.),

in this example: 100 Hz.

This pattern continues
        with less intensity
                into infinity...

Understanding The Sisters

(These notes correspond to wave numbers on previous page)

8.   This eighth harmonic is the same pitch class as the fundamental tone (Doe).
Notice that in the first octave of the harmonic series there is one unique tone: Doe {1}.
The second octave contains two tones: Doe and Sol {2, 3}. The third octave contains four
tones, which we refer to as the "Chord of Life": Doe, Mee, Sol & Ah {4, 5, 6, 7}.
This fourth octave contains eight harmonic tones.

9.   Frequency ratio is the inverse of the string length ratio: in Rae's case, each wave
is 1/9 string length and compared to the whole string vibrates a 9/1 frequency ratio.

10.   Notice Mee at 1000 Hz is double the frequency (one octave higher) of Mee at 500 Hz
(wave number 5).

11.   "Fu" is our name for the eleventh tone in the harmonic scale, unnamed and unavailable
in normal chromatic tuning.

12.   One octave above Sol at 600 Hz, thus 1200 Hz.

13.   "Mu" is our name for the thirteenth harmonic.

14.   This fourteenth wave is double the frequency of Ah at 700 Hz, thus 1400 Hz.

15.   Tee, with the frequency ratio of 15/1 compared to the fundamental tone, is accepted in
some Western music.

Two Perspectives

1. "Open string" harmonics.

2. "Fretted string" harmonics.

The Rippling Pool of Chapter 4 represents Open String Harmonics.

Song placed these ratios {1/1, 1/2, 1/3, 1/4...} (page 123)
in the vertical left-hand column of the Field of Numbers.
Along the horizontal top line Song placed equivalents of 1:
{1/1, 2/2, 4/4, 8/8...}.
Then he cross-referenced these
to reveal the fretted string harmonics within the Field.

Fretted string harmonics refer to shortening the full string.
In making the "Rimba" in Chapter 8,
Gim measured ratios from the Field of Numbers onto a single string.
Pinching the string at these harmonic points
effectively created shorter & shorter string lengths,
producing higher & higher tones.
Gim tuned his Rimba by ear.

Guitar fret placement can be measured in this same manner.
(See page 194)

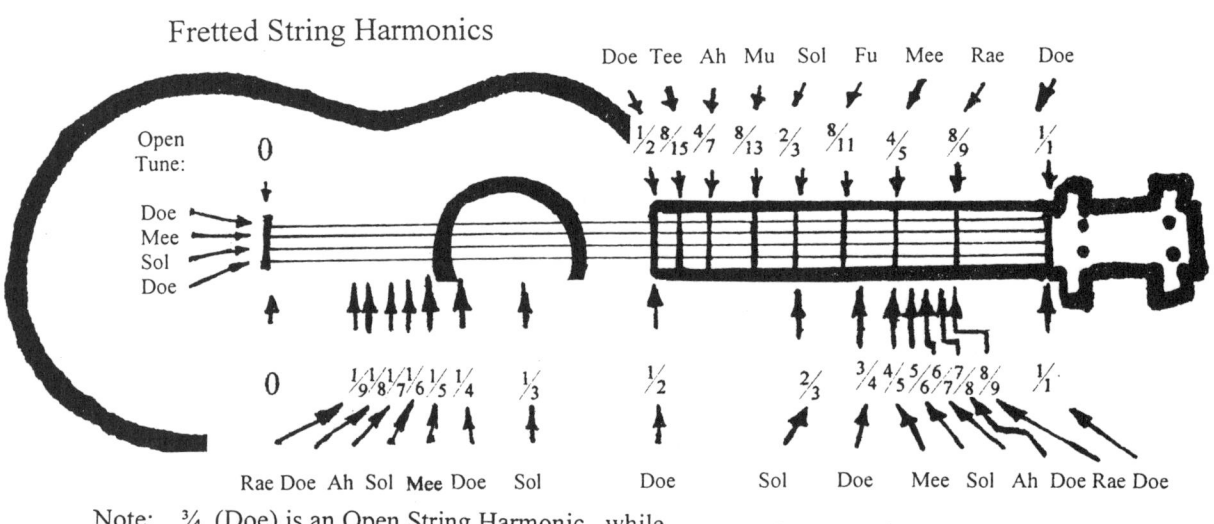

Fretted String Harmonics

Open String Harmonics

Note: ¾ (Doe) is an Open String Harmonic, while
       ¾ (Fa) is not a Fretted String Harmonic

192

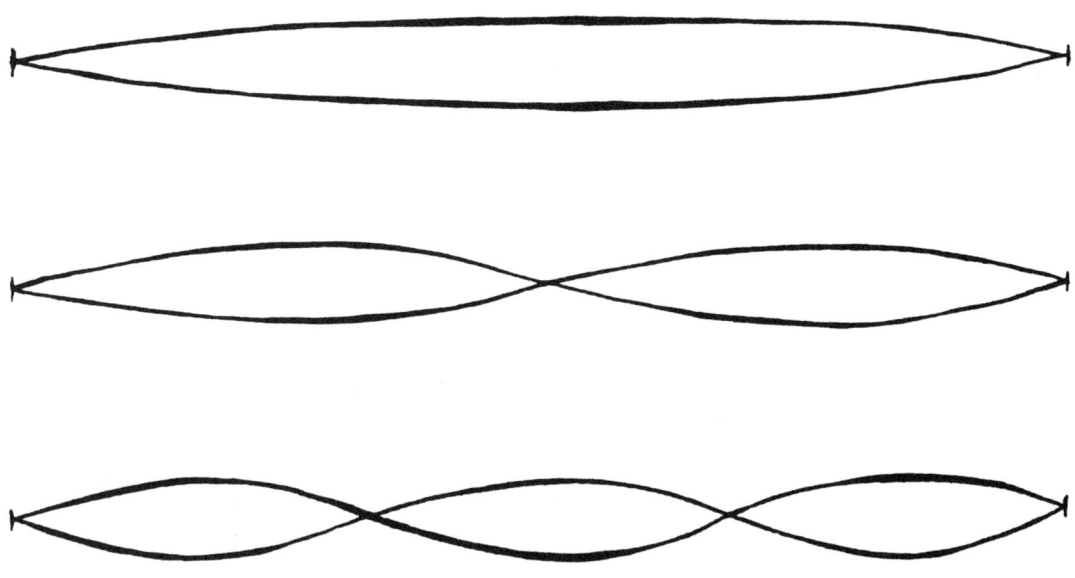

"In these
[String Theories proposed as Unified Field Theories in Physics]
the basic objects are not particles,
which occupy a single point in space
but things that have a length but no other dimension."

A Brief History of Time
by Stephen Hawking

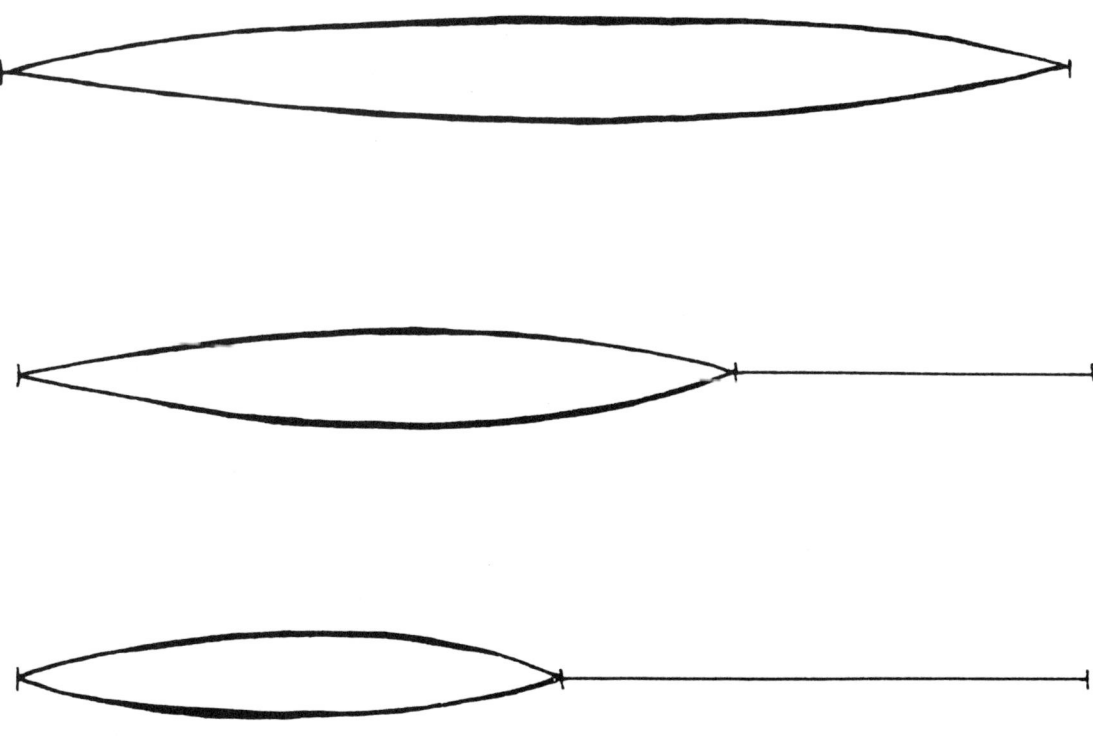

Fretted String Harmonics

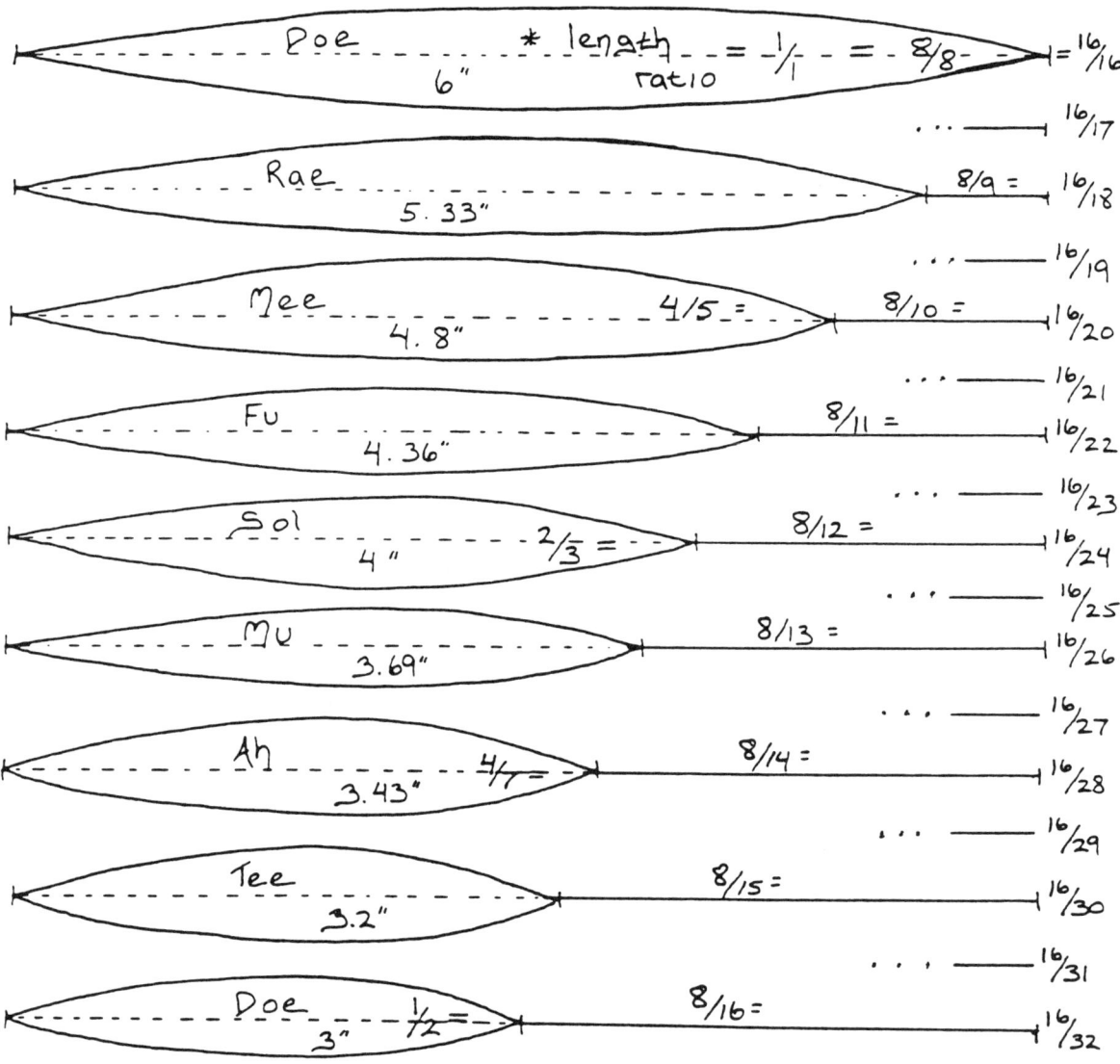

*The measurement for each harmonic fret location
is determined from multiplying the whole string length
by the string length ratio.
(see pg. 123)

194

Understanding Fretted String Harmonics

Frequency Ratios for Harmonic Overtone Series

Octave	Doe	Rae	Mee	Fu	Sol	Mu	Ah	Tee	Doe
1	1/1	9/8	5/4	11/8	3/2	13/8	7/4	15/8	2/1
2	2/1	9/4	5/2	11/4	3/1	13/4	7/2	15/4	4/1
3	4/1	9/2	5/1	11/2	6/1	13/2	7/1	15/2	8/1
4	8/1	9/1	10/1	11/1	12/1	13/1	14/1	15/1	16/1

The fourth octave can also be written:

|| 8 | 9 | 10 | 11 | 12 | 13 | 14 | 15 | 16

Compare the above with accepted "just" tuning below...
(modified from Pythagorean ratios)

Frequency Ratios for Just Tuning

Octave	Do	Re	Mi	Fa	Sol	La	Ti	Do
1	1/1	9/8	5/4	4/3	3/2	5/3	15/8	2/1
2	2/1	9/4	5/2	8/3	3/1	10/3	15/4	4/1
3	4/1	9/2	5/1	16/3	6/1	20/3	15/2	8/1
4	8/1	9/1	10/1	32/3	12/1	40/3	15/1	16/1

The fourth octave can also be written:

|| 8 | 9 | 10 | 10⅔ | 12 | 13⅓ | 15 | 16

Notice the absence of integers 11 (Fu), 13 (Mu), and 14 (Ah).

The frequency ratios in these charts can be flipped
to their reciprocals for string length ratios
(or column length ratios, in the case of a wind instrument).

Equitempered Scale:
Making Sense of Cents

<u>Search for Ah...</u> is a story about the differences between two sets of numbers:
the presence of 11, 13 and 14 in the harmonic overtone series,
and their absence in the accepted ratios of modern music.

Though the comparison is with what has evolved from Pythagorean ratios
(called "just" ratios), there is a third set of ratios even more commonly used today,
which is even further from nature's harmonic ratios.

Modern music is mostly "Equitempered".
This allows for shifting between keys without changing the ratios between each note.

To "create" 12 Equitempered notes between one octave note "C"
and double its frequency, the next higher octave note "C",
the formula "twelfth root of two" $\sqrt[12]{2}$ is used (1.059463094).
This means 12 different notes take root between the doubling of frequency
from "C" to "C". This is the accepted chromatic scale to which most pianos are tuned.

Between each note on a piano 100 "cents" have been assigned.
Thus, with 1200 cents per octave:

Equitempered Chromatic "C" Scale

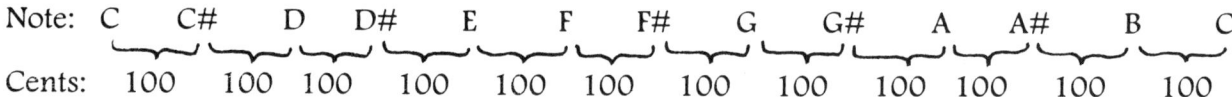

Note:	C	C#	D	D#	E	F	F#	G	G#	A	A#	B	C
Cents:		100	100	100	100	100	100	100	100	100	100	100	100

Equitempered Diatonic "C" Scale

Latin:	Do	Re	Mi	Fa	Sol	La	Ti	Do
Letter:	C	D	E	F	G	A	B	C
Ratio:	1/1	55/49	63/50	578/433	433/289	37/22	185/98	2/1
Cents:	200	200	100	200	200	200	100	

Tuning Adjustment:
Equitempered to Harmonic

A digitally tunable keyboard can be adjusted using cents:

$$1 \text{ cent} = \sqrt[1200]{2} = 1.00057779$$

We started with an assigned equitempered frequency,
then divided (down) or multiplied (up) by one cent
until the desired harmonic frequency was attained:

Keyboard note	Equitempered frequency (Hz)	Harmonic frequency(Hz)	Change in cents	Harmonic name
C	524	524	0	Doe
C#	554	556.75	+ 9	Shoooo
D	588	589.5	+ 4	Rae
D#	622	622.5	+ 1	Lao
E	660	655	- 13	Mee
F	698	720.5	+ 55	Fu
F#	740	753.25	+ 31	Sthee
G	784	786	+ 4	Sol
G#	830	818.75	- 24	Coo
A	880	851.5	- 57	Mu
A#	932	917	- 28	Ah
B	988	982.5	- 10	Tee

The chromatic scale has 12 tones per octave while a comparable harmonic scale has 16.
Thus in translating, 4 of the 16 harmonic tones get left out (Flaaa, P, Chew, Wa).
Notice: the major chord notes Do, Mi, Sol in just tuning on page 195 share ratios with
harmonics Doe, Mee, Sol while equitempered Mi (E) is off 13 cents and Sol (G) is off 4.

A harmonic keyboard should have 8 white keys per octave, instead of 7,
and 8 black keys, instead of 5.
A visual reference for each Doe would identify octaves.

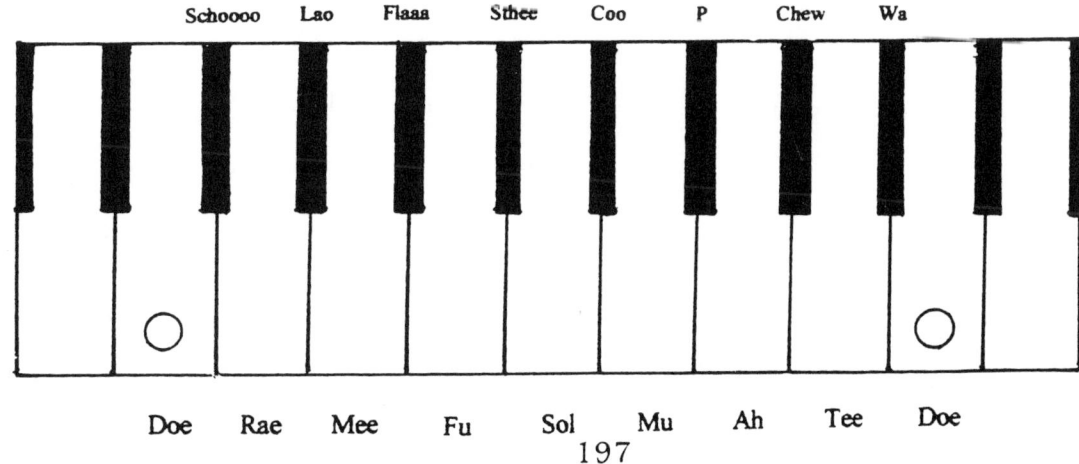

Schoooo   Lao   Flaaa   Sthee   Coo   P   Chew   Wa

Doe   Rae   Mee   Fu   Sol   Mu   Ah   Tee   Doe

Harmonic Series

*"...the frequency ratios of a note and its various harmonics
are represented by the complete sequence of numbers 2,3,4,5,6,7...
most of these harmonics are not represented
by notes on the Pythagorean scale at all."*

- Sir James Jeans; <u>Science and Music</u>

	#	Frequency Ratio	Name	Frequency	Octave
Actual Fundamental:	(1) . . .	1/8 . . .	Doe . . .	32.75 Hz. . . .	1
	2 . . .	2/8 . . .	Doe . . .	65.5 . . .	
	3	3/8	Sol	98.25	2
	4 . . .	4/8 . . .	Doe . . .	131 . . .	
	5	5/8	Mee	163.75	
	6	6/8	Sol	196.5	3
	7	7/8	Ah	229.25	
Chosen Fundamental *	8 . . .	8/8 . . .	Doe . . .	262 . . .	
	9	9/8	Rae	294.75	
	10	10/8	Mee	327.5	
	11	11/8	Fu	360.25	
	12	12/8	Sol	393	4
	13	13/8	Mu	425.75	
	14	14/8	Ah	458.5	
	15	15/8	Tee	491.25	
	16 . . .	16/8 . . .	Doe . . .	524 . . .	

* 262 Hz. is our chosen fundamental tone with a frequency ratio = 1/1.
Octave 4; (# 8 - 16), is the eight tone scale.

The fifth octave is a sixteen tone scale which includes the "sharps" (or "flats") precisely halfway (in Hertz) between the eight tones above. Odd-numbered tones (17,19,21,etc.) would be the black keys between each of the eight white keys on our theoretical piano.

#	Frequency Ratio	Name	Frequency	Octave
16 ...	16/8 ...	Doe ...	524 Hz. ...	
17	17/8	Schoooo	556.75	
18	18/8	Rae	589.5	
19	19/8	Lao	622.25	
20	20/8	Mee	655	
21	21/8	Flaaa	687.75	
22	22/8	Fu	720.5	
23	23/8	Sthee	753.25	
24	24/8	Sol	786	5
25	25/8	Coo	818.75	
26	26/8	Mu	851.5	
27	27/8	P	884.25	
28	28/8	Ah	917	
29	29/8	Chew	949.75	
30	30/8	Tee	982.5	
31	31/8	Wa	1015.25	
32 ...	32/8 ...	Doe ...	1048 ...	
				6

What Pythagoras Did:

$A^2 + B^2 = C^2$ is the "Pythagorean Theorem".
We have dubbed this "The Secret of Roofs" in chapter 3;
"Pytag-Orion Dream".

Pythagoras also experimented with vibrating string lengths, comparing consecutive integers and deriving the basic intervals used in modern Western music:

Did:

1	2	3	4	5
1/2	2/3	3/4	4/5	
(Do)	(Sol)	(Fa)	(Mi)	

His 1 to 2 ratio (1/2 & 2/1)
is the foundation for the "Octave Law" of halving and doubling.
His 2 to 3 ratio (2/3 & 3/2)
is nowadays called the
"perfect fifth" or "harmonic fifth".

The use of this "harmonic fifth", the 2/3 string length ratio, has evolved into what is now called the "circle of fifths". Though this method has been used in Western music to derive the chromatic scale, it is not exact.
By rotating the numbers
all the "major" scales almost unfold:

Poem to remember
order:

Father
Charles
Goes
Down
And
Ends
Battle

Moving
clockwise,
each
letter
is the
"harmonic
fifth"
of the
letter
before
it.

Notice: The bubbles in chapter 3 derive 13 ½ as the number for La,
but in order to make a simple ratio (see chart of "Fretted String Harmonics" page 195),
Western music has accepted 13 ⅓. Thus, La is accepted at a frequency ratio of 5/3.

What Pythagoras Didn't Do:

"Music in which a single tone predominates over all the others
is said to be 'tonal'...
this [single] tone is called the 'tonal center'."
<u>Harmonic Materials in Tonal Music</u>

If Pythagoras had instead compared each integer
with the fundamental tone (1),
he would have remained true to the natural laws of harmonics:

Didn't do:

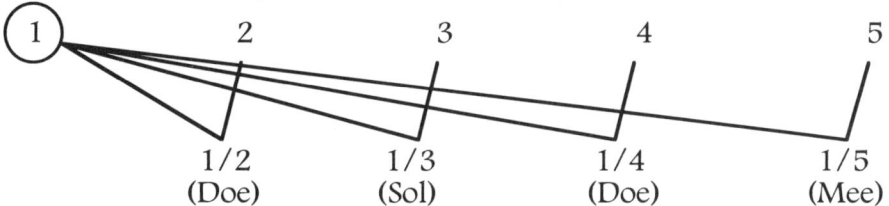

| 1 | 2 | 3 | 4 | 5 |

| 1/2 | 1/3 | 1/4 | 1/5 |
| (Doe) | (Sol) | (Doe) | (Mee) |

Notice:
using the octave law
and doubling these string length ratios,
only some of Pythagoras' ratios are found:

| 1/1 | 2/3 | 1/2 | 4/5 |
| (Doe) | (Sol) | (Doe) | (Mee) |

The 3/4 string length (Fa) is not a natural harmonic
of the fundamental tone 1/1 (Doe).
However, 1/2 string length
(the Fundamental Tone's first octave),
is a natural harmonic of the 3/4 string length:

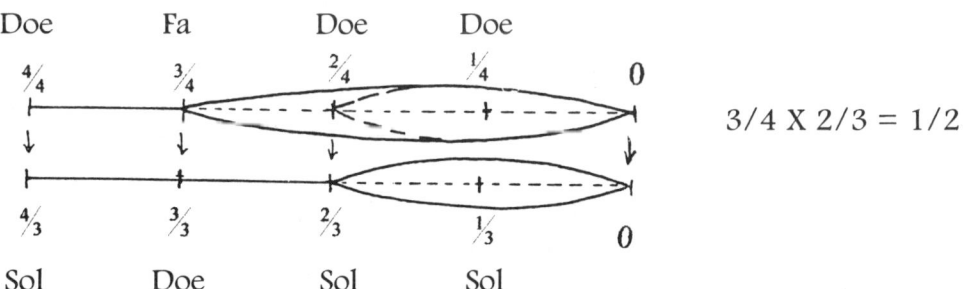

$$3/4 \times 2/3 = 1/2$$

This means that, according to the above definition of a tonal system,
in the presence of Fa, Doe no longer maintains her predominant position.
Fa takes over as Doe, forcing Doe to be Sol.

What Guido Did:

The naming of tones (Do Re Mi Fa Sol La Ti)
was initiated about 1040 A.D. by a monk; Guido of Arezzo.
He used the first syllable of each half line in a Sapphic hymn to John the Baptist.

"Ut queant laxis   Resonare fibris

Mira gestorum   Famuli tuorum,

Solve polluti   Labii reatum,

Sancte Iohannes."

(Ut Re Mi Fa Sol La Si)

Translation:

In order that the Family

may Become Quiet enough

to Resonate with the Loose Cord

& All Wonderful Things Done,

we need to Purify our Polluted Lips

& remove our Guilt,

O Saint John.

We drew from this tradition in naming the eight tones
in Search for Ah...

Guido also initiated use of "staff" lines for writing music.
He, as well, taught his students the diatonic scale
on the anatomy of his hand.

The Word In The Tone

The mathematics of harmonic overtones in <u>Search for Ah...</u>
came from a study of holography.
Holography manifests from a constant light reference which splits into two:
one remaining unchanged,
the other changing according to harmonic law.

"...invoking Brouwer's theorem
(in a continuous distortion of a system...
at least one point <u>must</u> remain unchanged. This point is the fixed point.)...
Through the fixed point, the frequency spectrum ...varies
- but relative to the frequency of the reference..."
<u>Shufflebrain, the Quest for the Hologramic Mind</u> by Paul Pietsch

The universality of harmonic overtones implied in <u>Search for Ah...</u>
is based on the idea that the universe and the mind functions as a hologram.
The original source light (Zero, the Void, the Way, God)
remains unchanged,
while the material universe evolves in harmony.

The single point requirement is the single tone
which began with the first existence of mass/energy.
This single tone, in alignment with the source light,
provides all the mathematical information needed to create the universe
in the harmonic overtone series.

"Nameless... is the source of creation.
But things have a mother and she has a name."
<u>The Way of Life Lao Tzu</u>   #1 & #42
translated by R. B. Blakney

"The Way begot one,
And the one, two;
Then the two begot three
And three, all else."

People have tuned into this constant universal vibration
by intoning a "Word" or "Name":
OM, RAM, AMEN, YAHWEH, JAH, ALLAH,
or another.

"Buried high in the right atrium, a minute knot of cells sets the heart's pace.
Called the sinus node, its sparks send electrical impulses racing through the heart
to other electrical cells woven throughout cardiac tissue.
In perfect rhythm each successively explodes.
The trail of electricity flashes so rapidly across the heart
that all its cells appear to beat as one."
- <u>The Incredible Machine: The Human Body</u>, National Geographic Books, 1986

From the Void (0)
comes the One tone (1)
then the many overtones:
(2,3,4,5,6,7...)

203

Field Of Numbers

In 1982 Mark C. Billington attempted to understand spiritual experiences through scientific language. This resulted in Mark graphing out a new perspective of the math of harmonics in his Field of Numbers.

The Field of Numbers defines harmonics by using the fundamental tone 1/1 as the fixed starting point.

Along the top horizontal of the Field of Numbers Mark applied the octave doubling rule to obtain equivalents of 1/1: 2/2, 4/4, 8/8...

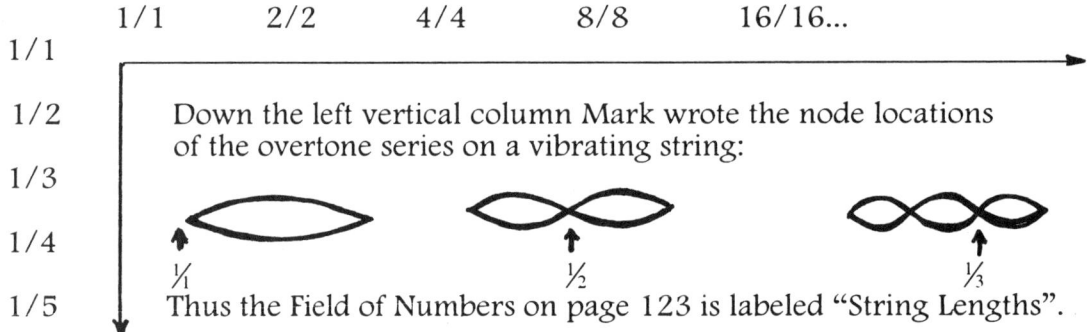

Down the left vertical column Mark wrote the node locations of the overtone series on a vibrating string:

Thus the Field of Numbers on page 123 is labeled "String Lengths".

The inverse of the ratios in the vertical column is the whole number sequence 1,2,3,4,5... The Field of Numbers presented this way would be labeled "Frequencies".
Example: Inverse of 2/3 string length would relate to 3/2 frequency.

Note that 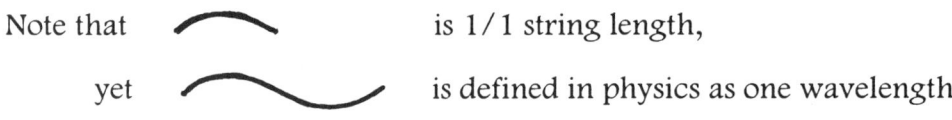 is 1/1 string length,

yet is defined in physics as one wavelength

thus one wavelength equals two string lengths.

The Field of Numbers can then be applied to such equations as $E = Mc^2$: $E = M(f\lambda)^2$

$$c = f\lambda$$

c = speed (of light, sound, whatever)
f = frequency
λ = wavelength (lambda)

Mark applies the Field of Numbers as a Unified Field Theory, also called Grand Unified Theory (G.U.T.) or Theory of Everything (T.O.E.): One set of numbers is required to fit all fields of science; mind or matter, quantum or relative.

Within the Field of Numbers, between the doublings and halvings of 1/1, there are sets, called Octaves, which are chords:

String lengths   {1/2, 1/3, 1/4} , {1/4, 1/5, 1/6, 1/7, 1/8}

Frequencies   {2, 3, 4} , {4, 5, 6, 7, 8}

The authors refer to   {4, 5, 6, 7} , (Doe, Mee, Sol, Ah) as "The Chord of Life".

The Chord Of Life

In music we can perceive several octaves. In light only one octave is visible.
Here the Chord of Life {4, 5, 6, 7} is found:

Sister	Color	Frequency	Wavelength	
	Infrared			
Doe		$\sim 4 \times 10^{14}$ Hz.	~ 700 nm	
	Red			color ranges
Rae				
	Orange			shown here
Mee		$\sim 5 \times 10^{14}$ Hz.	~ 600 nm	
	Yellow			are
Fu				
	Green			approximate
Sol		$\sim 6 \times 10^{14}$ Hz.	~ 500 nm	
	Blue			
Mu				
	Violet			
Ah		$\sim 7 \times 10^{14}$ Hz.	~ 400 nm	
Tee	Ultraviolet			

Authors claim no specific frequency as the universal Doe,
though Mark's theory requires one.
The Chord of Life (4,5,6,7) implies four primary colors rather than three.
These colors are found inside a water drop when a secondary rainbow is perceived,
as measured by Isaac Newton, between 50°- 54°.
This matches the angles in DNA
where the nitrogenous base ladder rungs connect to the double helix,
specific angles measured between
50° - 54° by Linus Pauling in 1956. Mark speculates further,
this match shows that harmony is required for healthy DNA.

In Biology, the most common elements found in flesh and bone
make up the Chord of Life (interpreted through the relationship of atomic numbers):

Hydrogen,	atomic number	1;	Doe
Carbon,	atomic number	6;	Sol
Nitrogen,	atomic number	7;	Ah
Oxygen,	atomic number	8;	Doe
Calcium,	atomic number	20;	Mee

Also note that elements are found to be harmonic through time as well.
This is revealed by the consistency of their "half life".

Mind Science

Brain waves are measured.
Different states of consciousness are associated with different frequencies:

Delta:
{1, 2, 3, 4} Hz. (cycles per second).
Deep, mostly dreamless sleep.

Theta: The Chord of Life
{4, 5, 6, 7, 8} Hz.
Sleeping dreams/waking dreams.
Associated with deep relaxation, increased suggestibility
and mental imagery.
In emergency induced adrenaline states we can achieve theta.

Alpha:
{8, 9, 10, 11, 12} Hz.
Awake, relaxed, meditative state.

Beta:
{13 and above...} Hz.
Normal waking state.
Higher frequencies are most often associated
with higher concentration or stimulation.

We "choose" how to divide the world.
An inch is divided harmonically:
{1 inch, 1/2 inch, 1/4 inch, 1/8, 1/16, 1/32...}
The "chromatic" scale is not.

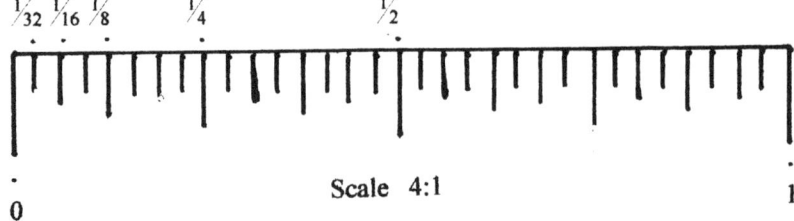

Scale 4:1

206

Computer Science

The binary system of computer language shown below
is another simple illustration of harmonic doubling:

Example of a binary number: 1100011

Translation:
The far right hand number represents either zero or one.
The next number to the left represents either zero or two.
The next number to the left equals either zero or four.
Each number to the left is either zero or the double (the next "octave")
of the number to its right (all doublings of one are Doe).
When added together, a base ten number is obtained:

1   1   0   0   0   1   1

64 + 32 + 0 + 0 + 0 + 2 + 1 = 99

A computer will then insert the character from its index
which is referred to by the number 99,
for instance, a period.

Or,
perhaps,
dot dot dot

. . .

Note the irony:
Zero represents something,
like the quiet string on which harmony plays:

The numbered musical waves
are energy dancing over the string,
which at rest, is Zero.
Only the Zero is an object.

Einstein's debated Zero Cosmological Constant
reveals that the energy density of the original vacuum
is emptiness;
Void.
Everything comes from nothing.

Compare to pages 30, 116, 117, 140, 161, 203 and 209.

Planetary Science
The Mystery of Titius-Bode "Law"

For thousands of years people have sought accurate explanations
of why planets orbit where they do.
Pythagoras tried to explain this with his musical ratios.
Astronomer Johannes Kepler (1571-1630) also proposed a chromatic relationship
among the orbits, called "music of the spheres".

In 1766, Wittenberg astronomer, Johann Daniel Titius,
translated a book written by Charles Bonnet, anonymously inserting his own formula.
Around 1772, while Titius wrote a second translation,
this time placing his numbers in a footnote,
Johann Elert Bode, of the Berlin Observatory, popularized Titius' math.
Titius-Bode law approximated the orbits of known planets.
In England, 1781, William Herschel's discovery of a planet,
near one of the Titius-Bode predicted orbits,
renewed belief in the validity of this so-called "law".
At first called Herschel, Bode later named the planet Uranus.
On New Year's Day, 1801, Giuseppe Piazzi, a Sicilian monk,
discovered a small planet he named Ceres.
This was the first and largest of the "asteroids", a term coined by Herschel,
found between Mars and Jupiter, also where predicted.
When Neptune and Pluto were discovered they eluded the Titius-Bode explanation,
causing interest in the "law" to wane.

The Titius-Bode numerical pattern is this:
Start the number set with zero: {0}, followed by three: {0, 3},
then the double of each previous number: {0, 3, 6, 12, 24...}.
Next add four: {4, 7, 10, 16, 28...}
then divide by ten: {.4, .7, 1.0, 1.6, 2.8...}.

Planet	Titius-Bode Prediction (A.U.)	*Actual Average Distance (A.U.)
Mercury	0.4	0.387
Venus	0.7	0.723
Earth	1.0	1.00
Mars	1.6	1.524
Ceres	2.8	2.767
Jupiter	5.2	5.203
Saturn	10.0	9.539
Uranus	19.6	19.191
Neptune	38.8	30.071
Pluto	77.2	39.158

One Astronomical Unit (A.U.) is the distance of Earth's average orbit from the Sun.
1 A.U. = $1.49597870 \times 10^{11}$ meters (about 93 million miles)
*from Academic American Encyclopedia (1987)

Orbital Harmony:
Understanding Titius-Bode Law

Equation: $r_H \approx (.3H_B + .4)$ A.U. (derived from Titius-Bode "law")

Symbols:
r_H = radius of planet's orbit from Sun (actual mean distance)
H_B = Harmonic Binary set: $\{0, 1, 2, 4, 8, 16...\}$
- Compare to Harmonic Sequence set: $H_S = \{1, 2, 3, 4, 5...\}$
Harmonic Dance set: $H_D = \{1, 2, 3, 4\}$
Harmonic Chord set: $H_C = \{1, 3, 5, 7...\}$
and Harmonic Chord of Life set: $H_L = \{4, 5, 6, 7\}$
A.U. = Astronomical Unit (about 93 million miles from Earth to Sun)

Note: .3 times the Harmonic set H_B exists because we have chosen the distance between our home and the Sun to be the Astronomical Unit (A.U.). If we use A.U. Modified (A.U.M.) where A.U.M. = .3 A.U. (a ring about 28 million miles from the Sun) then the Harmonic Binary set stands alone, without a multiplier: $r_H \approx (H_B + 4/3)$ A.U.M.
.4 A.U. (or 4/3 A.U.M.), which is Mercury's orbit at the zero Harmonic, is a function of the Sun's mass ($M_\odot$) and could probably be varied to accommodate central masses of other orbital systems.

Key to H_B:

H_B =		refers to		symbolized as	
=	0		Mercury	→	☿
=	1	→	Venus	→	♀
=	2	→	Earth	→	⊕
=	4	→	Mars	→	♂
=	8	→	Ceres	→	○
=	16	→	Jupiter	→	♃
=	32	→	Saturn	→	♄
=	64	→	Uranus	→	♅
=	96	→	* Neptune	→	♆
=	128	→	Pluto	→	♇

* Neptune is in sub-orbital degeneracy from the binary pattern:
$\{$Uranus, Neptune, Pluto$\} \rightarrow \{$Doe, Sol, Doe$\} = \{2, 3, 4\} = \{64, 96, 128\}$
predicting $\{19.6, 29.2, 38.8\}$ A.U.
Differences of predicted and actual $\{19.2, 30.1, 39.2\}$ A.U.
represent signal (harmonics) to noise (entropy) ratio.

Examples: A. Roughly how far is Mercury's average orbit from the Sun?
1. Use equation: $r_H \approx (.3H_B + .4)$ A.U.
2. Apply planet symbol to r.
3. Insert value for H_B
4. Insert value for A.U. (option)
5. Solve equation: $r_\text{☿} \approx [(.3)(0) + .4] \, 93 \times 10^6$ miles
$r_\text{☿} \approx 37.2 \times 10^6$ miles (.4 A.U.)

B. How far is Venus? $r_\text{♀} \approx (.3 + .4)$ A.U. = .7 A.U.

C. How far is Earth? $r_\text{⊕} \approx (.6 + .4)$ A.U. = 1.0 A.U.

Page Title Index

6. In the Green Chamber

7. Returns

Star Notes

"Can you Bind the Chains of the Pleiades
or Loose the Cords of Orion?"

- Job 38:31

1. Momma Bear, "Urr," is the Big Dipper
(Ursa Major, the Big Bear).

2. Brother Bear is "Bootes," known as "The Bear Chaser."

3. Baby Bear, "Browser," is the Little Dipper
(Ursa Minor, the Little Bear).

4. The North Star is Polaris, the fixed point.

5. "The Dangerous River" is traditionally "Draco the Dragon."

6. The "Boom-a-Rang" is Lyra the Lyre.

7. The "Path of the Boom-a-Rang" is the Precession Cycle
(rotation of Earth's axis: 26,000 years).

8. "King Art" is Cepheus, the King.

9. "Queen Omma" is Cassiopeia, the Queen.

10. "The Great Double Kite" or "Bird of the Spirit"
is Gemini, the Twins (Will is Castor, Flux is Pollux).

11. The "Bull-Head" (Pytag) is Taurus.

12. "The Sisters" are the Pleiades
(Subaru in Japanese).

13. "Yoti" is Canis Minor, the Little Dog.

14. "Seerius" is Canis Major, the Big Dog.
Sirius is the brightest visible star
in the Northern Hemisphere.

15. "Magic" is Monoceros, a Unicorn.

16. "The River of Life" is Eridanus, the River.

17. "The Chord of Life" is Auriga, the Charioteer.
Ah is Capella.

Glossary*

Chromatic:

Pertaining to chords or harmonies
based on nonharmonic tones.

Degeneracy:

To deteriorate.
Physics: Taking on several
discrete or distinct
values or states.
Etymology: To fall from one's
ancestral quality.

Gallumph:

The natural 4 beat run
of a long tailed bear
as differentiated from gallop,
a natural 3 beat gait of a horse.

Integrity:

Soundness, completeness, unity.
From "integer"; whole.

Synergy:

Etymology:
From Greek "sunergos": working together.

Biology:
The action of two or more substances, organs or organisms
to achieve an effect of which each is individually incapable.

Theology:
The doctrine that regeneration is effected by a combination
of human will & divine grace.

* adapted from American Heritage Dictionary (unabridged) and Oxford English Dictionary

About the Authors

Mark and Joe met in the winter of 1984/85 while working as professional ski patrollers
at Crystal Mountain in the Washington Cascades.
Early mornings after storms they used dynamite to control avalanches.
The rest of the day they worked on rescues and first aid.

During those long winter evenings Joe and Mark shared their stories:
In 1981 Mark had kayaked for six months between Seattle and Alaska.
In 1982, from travel journals, he wrote <u>I Can't See the Wind</u>.
Since 1982, Joe had worked for the Forest Service as a back-country ranger
in the Three Sisters Wilderness of Central Oregon.
From his photographs and poetry, Joe had compiled a book called <u>Mountain Notes</u>.

In 1991, Mark and Joe reunited on an island.
Joe told Mark: "I'm writing a story about the seven sisters;
Doe, Ray, Me, Fa, So, La, Tea and their brother, Song. "
Mark told Joe: "That family is dysfunctional."
Joe said: "What do you mean?"

Soon after that conversation, Joe asked The Evergreen State College professor, Terry Setter,
to sponsor a research project into Mark's harmonic theory.
This resulted in the writing of <u>Search for Ah...</u> ,
hand-crafting unique musical instruments and performing harmonic music.

Kristi's hobby has always been drawing.
She brought her talent to Joe's poetic goals and Mark's number goals
to help manifest <u>Search for Ah...</u>.
Mark and Kristi married in December, 1994.
Ammah is their daughter.

Currently Joe, Mark and Kristi are creating the sequel,
<u>Dance of the Superstring</u>.

Thanks

from Joe to:

Mom, Dad & my faithful brother John for all kinds of support;
Mark & Kristi for years of hard work;
Terry Setter for sponsoring this project from its inception;
Carolyn Forché for initiating my poetry on the path of extremes;
Maharaji for opening my senses to the Sacred;
All my teachers & friends for life.

from Mark:

Thanks folks
for genes, a brother,
food, shelter & love.

Thanks Kristi & Ammah
for love & support.

Thanks Joe for playing harmony with me.

Thanks God.

from Kristi:

I'm thanking Grandma & Grampy Blomgren
for showing me grace & strength.

Thanks to Mark & Ammah
for friendship & family coziness.

I want to thank Mom & Dad-in-Law
for love & hugs.

Thanks God.

217

Dance of the Superstring

Harmonics are overtones
flowing naturally from a fundamental tone.
Overtones dissipate into infinity, but
Dance can stabilize unfolding harmony
into sustaining creation.

Dance of the Superstring
follows the characters of Search for Ah...
through five days after the Tone Berry Jam.
The story explores Zero, as the "Nevermind"
and {1, 2, 3, 4} in the "Dance of the Superstring".
The "Chord of Life" {4, 5, 6, 7} brings surprises,
while Doe & her sisters {8 ~ 16}
join their cousins {odd numbers: 17 ~ 31}.

$$2H_D{}^2$$

Notes

"We dance round in a ring and suppose,
but the Secret sits in the middle and knows."

- Robert Frost

Notes

"True science to an ever-increasing degree discovers God
as though God were waiting behind each door opened by science."

- Pope Pius XII, 1951

Notes

"Science without religion is lame,
religion without science is blind."

- Albert Einstein

The Word in The Tone

The sword in the stone, the word in the tone.
The sword in the one, the word in the stone.
The sword in the tone, the word in the one.

"Why would you bother to have a brain that can attain spiritual experiences
if there were no spirituality in the world?
It wouldn't be adaptive."
- Karl Pribram

"Creation by the Word of God expresses God's absolute lordship and prepares
for the doctrine of creation out of nothing."
- annotation for Genesis 1:3-5 of The New Oxford Annotated Bible

"A non-zero vacuum energy density (cosmological constant) would have an obvious
and highly visible effect on the geometry of space and time."
- Larry Abbot

"I AM (YHWH) has sent me to you... 'this is my name forever;
and thus I am to be remembered throughout all generations.'"
- Exodus 3:14

"YHWH... had come to be regarded as too sacred to be pronounced...
and is entirely inappropriate for the Universal Faith of the Christian Church."
- from the preface to The New Oxford Annotated Bible

"In the beginning was the Word, and the Word was with God,
and the Word was God... All things were made by Him...
In Him was Life; and the Life was the Light of Men."
- John 1:1 - 1:14

"The AMEN is Jesus Christ."
- annotation for Revelations 3:14 in The New Oxford Annotated Bible

"That is why we utter AMEN through him, to the glory of God."
- 2 Corinthians 1:20

"kingdom: an area in which one thing is dominant"
- American Heritage Dictionary

"After all, it was said that a man who could repeat the sacred formula [Sufi: YA HU]
could even walk on the waves."
- Indries Shah

d

"There you have the three great Western religions; Judaism, Christianity and Islam -
and because the three of them have three different names for the same biblical god,
they can't get on together."
- Joseph Campbell in <u>The Power of Myth</u> by Bill Moyers

"The Word (or Name) is so secret that initiates are taught it one letter at a time.
First they [Freemasons] learn A, then O, then M, and finally I.
The Word is IAOM."
- <u>Big Secrets</u> by Poundstone

"The goal which all the Vedas declare, which all austerities aim at,
and which men desire when they lead a life of continence,
I will tell you briefly: it is OM.
This syllable OM is indeed Brahman. This syllable is the highest.
Whosoever knows this support is adored in the world of Brahma."
- <u>Katha Upanishad</u> 1, ii, 15-17

A Hindu greeting, "Namaste", means,
I honor that place in you, where if you are in that place in you,
and I am in that place in me, then we are One.

"Walk with the knowledge of that silence
while still singing the name of God."
- <u>Firelord</u> by Parke Godwin

<u>Notes</u>

"What is called science today consists of a haphazard heap of information
united by nothing."
- Leo Lolstoy

Notes

"...to insist that information and mass-energy are one and the same would quickly put the natural sciences in an untenable philosophical position."
- <u>Shufflebrain</u> by Paul Pietsch

8

Notes

"...a tape recording of such earth vibrations played back
at a speed far higher than the recording speed...
the earthquake had set the earth ringing like a bell!"
- Acoustic Techniques for Home and Studio by F. Alton Everest

Notes

"sympathy n. 6. *physics* a relation or harmony between bodies
of such a nature that vibrations in one
cause sympathetic vibrations in the other or others"
- Webster's New World Dictionary

Notes

"cohesion; the mutual attraction
by which elements of a body are held together...
waves with a continuous relationship among phases"
- American Heritage Dictionary

k

Notes

"If a system at equilibrium is subjected to a stress...
the system will react in a way that tends to relieve the stress."
- La Chatelier Principle

Notes

"However, if we do discover a complete theory,
it should in time be understood in broad principle
by everyone, not just a few scientists."
- <u>A Brief History of Time</u> by Stephen Hawking